GARDEN ROOMS

Time-Life Books is a division of Time Life Inc.

TIME LIFE INC.

PRESIDENT AND CEO: George Artandi

TIME-LIFE CUSTOM PUBLISHING

VICE PRESIDENT AND PUBLISHER: Terry Newell
Vice President of Sales and Marketing: Neil Levin
Director of Acquisitions: Jennifer Pearce
Editor: Linda Bellamy
Production Manager: Carolyn Clark
Quality Assurance Manager: James D. King

Book Design: Kathleen Mallow

First printing. Printed in U.S.A.
Pre-Press Services, Time-Life Imaging Center

TIME-LIFE is a trademark of Time Warner Inc. U.S.A.

Library of Congress Cataloging-in-Publication Data

Erler, Catriona T.
Garden rooms : creating and decorating outdoor garden spaces / by Catriona Tudor Erler; with photographs by James Walsh Erler and Catriona Erler.
p. cm.
Includes index.
ISBN 0-7370-0601-3 (alk. paper)
1. Landscape gardening. 2. Garden rooms. 3. Garden ornaments and furniture.
I. Title.
SB473.E753   1999   747'.98—dc21   98-52935   CIP

Books produced by Time-Life Custom Publishing are available at a special bulk discount for promotional and premium use. Custom adaptations can also be created to meet your specific marketing goals. Call 1-800-323-5255.

GARDEN ROOMS

Create and Decorate Outdoor Garden Spaces

by Catriona Tudor Erler

TIME-LIFE BOOKS

ALEXANDRIA, VIRGINIA

CONTENTS

PART ONE

Creating GARDEN ROOMS

Your garden should make as important a contribution to your home life as your house. A small garden will feel much larger if it is divided into different areas, each with a particular function or use. Likewise, a large garden divided into smaller rooms becomes a fascinating place to explore, with delightful surprises around each bend in the path.

SHELTERED BY TREES AND SURROUNDED BY FLOWERS, THIS NOOK IS A SPECIAL LITTLE GARDEN ROOM WITHIN A LARGER SPACE.

CHAPTER ONE

Rooms for Gardens Large and Small

The concept of garden rooms is centuries old. The terraced Italian gardens built in the 16th century were a series of rooms that ranged from formal to informal; the closer to the house, the more formal the design. The French adapted the idea to their flat terrain, creating rooms defined by parterres, walls, and paving, and linked by alleés and grand canals. Across the Channel, the English also designed their gardens as a series of rooms divided by hedges, walls, and parterres, and linked by paths.

The American colonists brought the concept of garden rooms with them from England. In the early years of simple survival, garden rooms were primarily vegetable and herb gardens enclosed with a fence made of palings to keep out chickens and roaming livestock. As life got easier, the gardens became more ornamental. The American tradition of garden rooms continued until the early 19th century, when the naturalistic garden style pioneered by Lancelot "Capability" Brown and his colleagues in England became popular.

We owe the modern garden room to Gertrude Jekyll, the well-known English garden writer and designer who lived and worked at the turn of this

LEFT: A PICKET FENCE WITH A SIMPLE ARBOR OVER THE GATE DEFINES THE BOUNDARIES OF THIS GARDEN-WITHIN-A-GARDEN. ABOVE: THE BOXWOOD HEDGES THAT FRAME THE VEGETABLE BEDS TRANSFORM THIS GARDEN FROM A UTILITARIAN PATCH OF GROUND TO A GARDEN ROOM.

century. Her designs for large country gardens in the south of England included dramatic elements, such as long views along a main garden axis and fabulous perennial borders, as well as small, more intimate garden rooms, each with a different theme.

Today most people don't have estates with acres of land to devote to gardens. Nevertheless, the opportunities for garden rooms abound, even on a very small property. For example, the patch of ground in front of your house is a garden room that serves as the foyer to your home. The space between your home and the house next door has the poten-

tial to be a room, or even several rooms, each special in its own way.

A patio or deck functions as a garden room, set apart visually from the rest of the garden by the floor or surface covering. We also perceive it as a distinct space because we use it for sitting or dining. With a little landscaping creativity—such as building an arbor over the spot, adding pretty pots full of flowers, or planting around the perimeter to create a physical barrier—you can emphasize the distinction, making the patio or deck a special room in your garden.

In addition to making your garden more inter-

ALTHOUGH PHYSICALLY OUT IN THE OPEN, THIS BRICK PATIO FEELS PRIVATE AND SECLUDED BECAUSE IT IS SURROUNDED ON THREE SIDES BY LOW-GROWING SHRUBS. THE ATTRACTIVE, COMFORTABLE FURNITURE ENCOURAGES GUESTS TO SETTLE IN FOR A LONG VISIT.

esting, dividing the land into separate rooms can increase the usable space on your property. When a backyard is simply a patch of lawn surrounded by shrubs, there's not much value in the space except as an area for children to play. Instead, you could have a small vegetable garden, a bit of lawn for the children to romp, and a small paved area (perhaps at the far end of the lawn) large enough for a couple of chairs. Link the spaces with paths, and suddenly you've got a garden where you can take walks, sit and relax, harvest fresh vegetables, and enjoy watching the children play.

Dividing Small Spaces

Because many residential lots today are small, we tend to assume there isn't enough room to divide up the garden space. In most cases, there's more room than you might think. Keep in mind that it isn't necessary to enclose a space completely to make it a separate room, indoors or out. For example, many homes are laid out in what's called an open floor plan: Rooms merge with each other, and the divisions are visual or even psychological. A living room and dining room may be in one large, open space; to distinguish the two areas, the floor of the living room might be carpeted while the dining room space

WHILE THE HIGH WALL COVERED WITH ES-
PALIERED ORANGE TREES DEFINES THE BOR-
DERS OF THIS GARDEN ROOM IN LA JOLLA,
CALIFORNIA, EACH SQUARE RAISED BED IS
PERCEIVED AS A MINIATURE ROOM WITHIN
THE LARGER SPACE.

might have a wooden floor. In the kitchen, a counter might serve as a partition between the breakfast nook and the cooking area, and the family room is set apart by a step down from this space. Changes in floor covering, different levels, and partitions all serve to divide the space while also keeping it open.

These same principles apply in the garden. A low hedge, a path, a border of flowers, or a change in sur-

face—for example, from grass to ground cover or paving are all ways of setting one space apart from another and providing a sense of enclosure.

In fact, it is a curious paradox that a small space will seem larger if it is divided into different areas. Visual interruptions expand the sense of space; if there's a bit more garden around the corner or out of the line of vision, you'll have the feeling that the overall garden is larger. In addition, it is more appealing if you cannot see everything at once. There's a compelling charm and a delightful sense of mystery about a garden that promises visual treats just around the corner, on the other side of the hedge, or just over the rise.

Making the Most of Small Gardens

Small gardens don't need to feel cramped. By using a few design tricks, you can make a garden seem much larger than it really is.

Objects that are far away normally look smaller to us than those that are up close. You can use this sense of perspective to make the distance in your garden appear greater. For example, try making a path gradually narrower as it moves away from the house toward the back of the garden. If you're paving with steppingstones, choose smaller stones for the portion of the path that's farthest away. If you're building a wall or fence around your property, make it a little shorter at the far end of the gar-

A TALL EUGENIA HEDGE PROTECTS THIS SMALL FRONT GARDEN FROM THE STREET. ALTHOUGH ONLY ABOUT 15 FEET SQUARE, THIS LITTLE GARDEN ROOM SUPPORTS A HOST OF PLANTS AS WELL AS A SMALL POND AND FOUNTAIN.

den. The exaggerated perspective will expand your property visually.

You can use the same trick when building a brick patio in a narrow garden. Begin closest to the house with standard 8-inch-long bricks set in a running pattern facing the back of the garden. As you get closer to the far end, gradually reduce the length of the bricks until they are about half or one-third the normal size. The back boundary will look farther away than it actually is.

A flat, grassy area looks larger if it is lower than the surrounding garden. If you can't afford to regrade the lawn to create a sunken area, make raised beds around it and place a bench on top of one of the beds so you can enjoy the perspective from above.

A change in level also makes an entire garden feel larger. Not only does it provide visual variety, in some cases it adds interest by keeping the viewer guessing. If your property is small and flat, for instance, you might consider bringing in soil to create a raised mound that obscures part of the garden; when the eye cannot see everything at once, the viewer will assume there is much more. If you also plant a tree on top of the mound, then surround it with low-growing shrubs, the short shrubs will make the tree appear taller.

Another way to block the view of an entire gar-

den is with a trellis or screen of shrubs. Use these partitions to emphasize diagonal lines, which add a sense of movement to the design and draw the eye down the greatest distance. For instance, plant a hedge or build a trellis across a long, narrow garden about two-thirds down the length. You'll make the area in front of the screen more pleasing, and you

---

THIS SUNDIAL SET AT THE END OF THE SHORT PATH DRAWS THE EYE, ADDING A POINT OF IN-TEREST IN THE GARDEN. BEHIND, THE FENCE TOPPED WITH TRELLIS PROVIDES PRIVACY WITH-OUT LOOMING AS AN OPPRESSIVE FEATURE.

can create a secret garden or work space behind the partition.

Your garden will also appear larger if the eye is encouraged to move from one focal point to another. In a small front garden with a path leading straight to the front door, you can add interest by building a steppingstone path that branches off from the main path. Put something decorative at the end of the secondary path, such as a sundial, birdbath, statue, or bench, so that it has a destination.

Now the eye will be drawn to both the front door and the sundial or other point of interest.

Keeping a Small Garden in Scale

In a small garden, choose plants that are in scale with the surroundings. Many miniature varieties of large plants are now available that are suitable for tiny garden plots. For example, there is a dwarf version of the majestic southern magnolia (*Magnolia grandiflora*) called 'Little Gem'. Instead of reaching

a mature height of 20 to 60 feet with a spread of 50 feet, 'Little Gem' tops out at 20 feet tall with a 10-foot spread. The flowering dogwood *Cornus florida* 'Rainbow' is another compact introduction that grows to about 10 feet tall—half the height of the species—and only 8 feet wide.

Use these and other dwarf varieties of trees and shrubs as specimen plants in a small garden. These larger plants can also serve as a point of reference for the rest of the plantings in a small garden. For example, the largest tree might be the dwarf southern magnolia. Even though the tree will remain relatively small, it will seem large next to smaller shrubs and perennials.

Other garden features should also be in proportion to their surroundings. For a steppingstone path, use small stones; large stones can look out of place in a small area. Choose garden furniture that fits the available space comfortably, and pick ornaments that make attractive focal points without dwarfing everything nearby.

While you don't want plants or ornaments that are too large for the space, you should also avoid filling the garden with too many small items. If you do, you run the risk of creating meaningless clutter that tires the viewer. Even a small garden needs a substantial focal point and a few hefty plants to add bulk to the design. Mix large plants and ornaments (relative to the space available) with smaller ones to create a pleasing sense of proportion and contrast.

Front Garden Rooms

Think of the front of your property as at least one additional garden room. Whether you decide to leave it open to the street or enclose it to create a private space, remember that this is the first impression visitors will have of your home. Use your front garden to set the tone of your home and to make guests feel welcome.

A comfortably wide and evenly paved path makes it easy for people to reach your front door. Make sure it's well lighted for nighttime visitors, and keep the path clear of plants. Although it's charming for plants to spill onto paths to soften their edges, don't let them encroach so much that there isn't room to walk.

Subtle details can also help make visitors feel welcome. For example, try planting scented herbs or plants with a sweet perfume next to the front door. People will enjoy the pleasant fragrances as they wait for you to open the door, and they will eventually associate those scents with you and your warm hospitality.

If you have a front porch, treat it as a special garden room. Consider growing vines up the support posts and hanging baskets of colorful flowers or ferns from the ceiling or porch eaves. Fill the corners of your porch with pots overflowing with plants to create a lush-looking bower. Add an inviting chair or bench or a swing so that people will want to sit on the front porch on summer evenings and

CLEAN LINES AND A SIMPLE, GEOMETRIC PATTERN MAKE THIS SMALL GARDEN PARTICULARLY PLEASING. THE STEEP SLOPE TO THE RIGHT FUNCTIONS AS A GARDEN BOUNDARY, GIVING THE SENSE OF A SUNKEN GARDEN SET APART AS A SPECIAL PLACE TO RELAX.

relax or greet the neighbors as they stroll past.

Most Americans leave their front garden exposed to the street and use trees and shrubs as foundation plantings next to the house. If you have a small yard without a private garden in back, consider moving the foundation plantings to the perimeter of your property to create an enclosed space where you can sit without being watched by the world. Alternatively, you could plant a hedge or add a wall or fence along the property line. You might be surprised to find that the unused space in the front has now become a valued and treasured part of your garden.

In some neighborhoods an enclosed front garden would look out of place or give an unfriendly impression. If that's the case where you live, you can still create a sense of enclosure by extending the foundation planting beds so they curve outward toward the front, like arms reaching out to encircle visitors in a hug. Or you could put a low border of plants along the perimeter of your property to increase the sense of privacy without completely shutting out the neighborhood.

THE PLANT-FESTOONED PICKET FENCE SURROUNDING THIS FRONT GARDEN PROVIDES A PLEASING SENSE OF ENCLOSURE AND PRIVACY. PLANTED IN THE COTTAGE GARDEN STYLE, THIS GARDEN HAS THE DELIGHTFUL TENSION CREATED BY "ORDERED CHAOS."

Side Garden Rooms

The space between houses can be challenging to landscape, particularly if it is long and narrow and shady for much of the day. Often this area is ignored altogether, or used for storing trash cans or miscellaneous items.

You may decide to make the space into a workroom, complete with storage shelves for pots and a bench or table for potting and other garden chores. Or, with some imagination, you can transform the space into a charming garden room, or at least a pretty passage that links the front and back gardens.

If the space is very narrow, try vertical gardening. Grow vines up the walls or fences, or espalier trees or shrubs to keep them from growing outward and encroaching on the limited space. Plant in layers to give a richer, more lush effect. In a narrow bed, for example, start at the back with a vine, tall shrub, or small tree. Place something shorter in front (you may need to stagger the plants to provide room for all the roots), and finish off with a ground cover.

For a low-maintenance design, particularly in a dry climate where water is at a premium, consider creating a dry streambed that runs the length of the narrow space. Choose a fine gray stone for the meandering stream (which can double as a path), and then create the stream bank with coarser stones in a

A PAIR OF ATLAS CEDAR TREES (*Cedrus atlantica* 'GLAUCA PENDULA') TRAINED TO FORM AN ARCH FRAMES THE ENTRANCE TO THIS SHADY GLADE WHERE A TIERED FOUNTAIN IS THE CENTRAL FEATURE.

contrasting color. To add bulk to the design, place a few large stones where they will enhance the illusion of a river or stream, and plant a shrub or two and a small tree for a cooling green touch.

If you have a yen for a secret garden room where you can retreat from life's daily demands, the space at the side of the house may be the perfect spot. If it's narrow, it will already have a sense of enclosure, but you may still want to plant a hedge or a screen of trees or build a trellis to create additional privacy. Consider installing a fountain or small pool to make the room more alluring, and furnish it with a comfortable seat or two.

Large Gardens

Too much space can be as problematic as too little. While wide-open vistas that stretch across the horizon are appealing, people also yearn for small, intimate spaces. If you have a large property, it's fine to show off the abundance of land with open spaces and long vistas. However, you should also set aside space for smaller garden rooms where people can retreat and enjoy the intricate details of plantings and ornaments.

Phillip Watson, a landscape designer based in Fredericksburg, Virginia, thinks of garden rooms in terms of vignettes. "In a large garden, I plan lots of vignettes," he says. "I determine the size of the vignette by what you can see in a wide-angle camera lens, because that's about how much the eye can take in. The exception is if you have a vantage point high enough or far enough away to take in more."

As an aid in dividing the space, you might have a long, open avenue that runs the length of the property, with smaller rooms branching off. For example, at the historic Oatlands Plantation in Leesburg, Virginia, George Carter designed his 4-acre garden as a series of terraces that branch off from the central walkway, which slopes down the hillside. As is typical of early 19th-century American gardens, symmetrical pairs of plantings flank the walkway at each level, providing definition and framing the view across each terraced garden room.

Filoli, the famous garden planted in the early part of this century in Woodside, California, near San Francisco, is another excellent example of a large garden with smaller garden rooms full of unexpected treasures. Now open to the public, the gardens grace 16 acres of the estate. Some rooms are vast, with wide, flat vistas that rest the eye and contrast with the wild, hilly California scenery beyond the manicured lawns, canal-like pools, and clipped hedges. Other rooms are more intimate, surrounded by a screen of trees and defined by clipped boxwood parterres. These smaller garden rooms generally have themes, such as the rose garden, the Chartres Cathedral Window Garden (designed with parterres and annuals to resemble the stained-glass windows at Chartres Cathedral in France), the knot gardens, and the annual borders. At Filoli, the large, open spaces are pleasant foils for the smaller gardens.

While it is perfectly fine—in fact, desirable—for each garden room to be different from all the

A SERPENTINE PATH THAT LOOPS DOWN THE LENGTH OF THIS NARROW CANYON GARDEN DIVIDES THE SPACE INTO LAWN-PAVED GARDEN ROOMS.

others, you want to create a natural flow between the rooms. Link them with paths that beckon you to explore, doorways that invite you to pass over the threshold, and pergolas that draw you through the space. To unify the design, choose a plant theme, such as boxwood parterres or yew hedges, that is repeated throughout the garden. This repetition contributes a comforting sense of continuity amid all the diversity.

Garden rooms have a definite allure because they provide an opportunity for exploration and discovery. As novelist H. E. Bates wrote in his collection of essays titled *A Love of Flowers:* "The garden within a garden: the idea at once excites and satisfies. The eye is led down a path, over steps, cunningly around corners, past concealments of walls and shrubs, until at last a new stage, set with its scene of leaf and flower, is reached. Then is the garden never seen in its entirety at one time. There is always something hidden that leads us on. Always there is that most seductive question—what is around the corner, down the steps or beyond the tree?"

CHAPTER TWO

Designing Rooms for Different Uses

Your garden has the potential to increase the living space of your home significantly. However, all that extra square footage will be wasted if you don't create an environment where you want to spend time.

The average suburban garden—with pavement near the house that leads to a grassy area surrounded by a narrow border of shrubs—has the same potential for usable living and working space as an office building that can be subdivided to suit the needs of its occupants. Just as you divide your home or office into different rooms for different uses, think about creating areas in your garden for specific activities. You may want a large, open space, like an indoor family room, where people can enjoy lots of different activities. But don't overlook the need for small, intimate places, too.

Your goal is to create rooms that will encourage everyone in your family to use the garden space and to enhance the quality of time they spend there.

Garden Rooms for Outdoor Activities

As you plan how you will divide the space in your garden to create different rooms, think about your family's needs.

If you have small children, perhaps you want to designate a playroom area, complete with a swing set, sandbox, and jungle gym. You might even include a paved path to serve as a "highway" for tricycles and other wheeled toys. Ideally the spot should be away from the street and visible from the house so you can keep an eye on the little ones. Avoid plants with thorns that could hurt the children, as well as fragile plants that could be trampled or easily broken.

For a "family room," allow space for an open, level lawn where children and grownups can kick a ball around or play croquet, badminton, or volley-

A ROSE-COVERED PERGOLA ARCHING OVER THIS STONE PATH DRAWS THE EYE AND THE MIND THROUGH THE GARDEN TO A FLOWERY BOWER FURNISHED WITH A COMFORTABLE WICKER CHAIR.

ball; an avid golfer might appreciate an area to practice putting. In this case, the lawn is part of a specific plan for family use, not the default landscape option chosen by most homeowners to cover bare ground around their property. To make life simpler, keep delicate plants away from this space so you don't have to constantly admonish people to "stay out of the beds and don't let the ball bounce on my prize delphinium."

If dining alfresco appeals to you, you may want to create an outdoor dining room furnished with a table and comfortable chairs. Whether you opt for a deck or a patio, make sure the space is large enough to comfortably accommodate your family and guests. For convenience, locate this outdoor room as close to the kitchen as possible. If the meal you're most likely to eat outside is breakfast or brunch, try to find a spot facing east to catch the morning sun. If evening meals are your preference, site the room on the south or west side of the house so you can enjoy the late-afternoon sun. In hot climates, use a vine-covered arbor to create a leafy bower with dappled

TOP: EQUIPPED WITH AN
OVERHEAD HEATER AND
LOCATED NEAR THE KITCHEN,
THIS ARBOR-COVERED PATIO
IS IDEAL FOR OUTDOOR
DINING, EVEN WHEN THERE
IS A CHILLY NIP IN THE AIR.
RIGHT: A TRADITIONAL
GARDEN ROOM DEVOTED TO
HERBS. LEFT: AN ARCED
PERENNIAL BORDER ENCIR-
CLES A TINY GARDEN ROOM.

sunlight. Decorate the paved space with pots and hanging baskets filled with scented flowers to add to the pleasure of dining outside.

Another garden room option is a formal sitting room. An herb or rose garden laid out in a geometric pattern is ideal for such a room. Furnish it with a bench, and enjoy sitting among the scented plants meditating on the pleasing order and symmetry.

If you have the space, think about creating a secret garden room where you can retreat with a cup of coffee and a good book. A corner of an asymmetrical lot or the far end of the garden is ideal for a qui-

et, private space. Another possible site for a secret garden is the narrow space at the side of the house. Use your imagination to transform it into a magical place where you'll want to go often. If the area you choose for a secret garden is in the open, encircle it with a hedge for privacy, or screen it from view with latticework. Provide a comfortable chair, and if your budget allows, install a small fountain so you can enjoy the soothing sound of falling water.

A kitchen garden is a joy for those who combine a love of gardening with a love of cooking. Although utilitarian, this space doesn't have to be unattractive.

Be creative in mixing vegetables with edible flowers. Or take a tip from the French, who create beautiful potager gardens in which the vegetables are planted in geometric patterns that emphasize the unusual forms and colors of the different plants. For added structure, outline your potager beds with low boxwood hedges or an edible low-growing plant.

For those who want to take walks in the garden, plan the landscape with rooms for strolling, and design the paths so they beckon visitors to move from one space to another *(see Chapter 6)*. To increase the walking distance in a small garden, allow the paths to connect with each other. Discourage people from cutting the corners by installing dense plantings that hide other paths nearby, and provide new views or points of interest around each bend and corner.

Finally, if you're an avid gardener, you may want a workroom hidden from view where you can raise seedlings, repot plants, store equipment, or keep a compost heap. This area may actually be a room with walls and a ceiling if you have a greenhouse, potting shed, or lath house. Otherwise, you may simply designate an out-of-the way area and screen it from view with shrubs or other plants, or

LEFT: YOU DON'T NEED A LOT OF SPACE TO PLANT A HERB GARDEN. ABOVE: THE GARDEN TOOLS HUNG ON THIS STORAGE SHED ARE BOTH CONVENIENT TO ACCESS AND DECORATIVE.

hide it behind a fence, wall, or trellis. This utility area can be as important to a gardener as a workshop is to a woodworking hobbyist.

Plant Themes or Collections

Something in human nature drives us to collect, and the plant kingdom offers wonderful opportunities to amass a wide variety of plants from particular families or genera. Whatever the collector's passion—be it roses, ferns, iris, orchids, hollies, scented geraniums, cacti, daylilies, or any other plant group—the goal generally is to have the widest possible selection of plants, including the most rare and unusual as well as the most recent introductions.

A plant collector has two options for displaying the treasures: to spread the plants throughout the garden, integrating them into the general decor, or to set aside a space or garden room to showcase the entire group. Of course, the advantage of keeping the collection together is that the wonderful range of plants can be seen in one place. However, there is no need to have a valuable collection of plants look

THIS VIBRANT COLLECTION OF HOT-COLORED AZALEAS IS A DYNAMIC FOCAL POINT IN THE GARDEN WHEN THEY ARE IN FULL BLOOM. OUT OF SEASON THEY ARE A USEFUL SCREEN OF FOLIAGE.

like the bargain shelf at a discount home center. To show off your plants to best effect, give them the right framework.

For example, you might incorporate a fern collection into a woodland garden, combined with other shade-loving plants; the ferns are still the focus, but you are displaying them in context. Show off the many variations in the primrose family by planting them along a stream or around a pond with other plants that need lots of moisture.

Massed beds of bearded iris look fantastic when they are in full bloom, and it's a treat to wander among them, marveling at the infinite variety of color combinations available in these rainbow flowers. But once their bloom is finished, iris are boring. To extend the season of interest, interplant iris with daylilies, or sow the seeds of an annual flower such as cosmos or larkspur among the plants.

As early as 600 B.C. the Greek poetess Sappho dubbed the rose "the queen of flowers," and with good reason. However, a rose blossom is a lot prettier than the bush. You can make a rose garden more attractive by planting beds in geometric shapes to create an overall pattern. Outline the beds with boxwood to frame the plants, or edge them with stone, brick, or a low-growing plant such as sweet alyssum, thrift, or Artemisia 'Silver Mound'. Create an arched frame covered with climbing roses in the center of the garden (see Chapter 9) to add height to the composition, and build an arbor or pergola at one end to support additional ramblers. Grow more climbers up rose pillars or pyramids in the center of the beds, and cover all the bare ground around the rose bushes with a pretty, low-growing ground cover.

In the introduction to her book *Color Schemes for the Flower Garden*, Gertrude Jekyll, the renowned 19th-century British garden designer, wrote: "I am strongly of opinion that the possession of a quantity of plants, however good the plants may be themselves and however ample their number, does not make a garden; it only makes a collection. Having got the plants, the great thing is to use them with careful selection and definite intention. … Use the plants [so] that they shall form beautiful pictures."

Color Themes

Color is a powerful force in our lives. Some colors, such as bold reds and oranges, stimulate and excite us; yellow is a cheerful color, reminding us of sunshine. Other colors are soothing. For example, pinks and blues tend to have a calming effect, and a garden masterfully composed of different shades of green is generally a restful place to be. Gray is easy on the eyes and is a great color to have by the sea where it eases the glare of light reflected off the water. It also moderates competing colors: put gray foliage between two flower colors that fight each other, and the battle will cease. White flowers, which intensify the perceived color of adjacent flowers, can add sparkle to a garden if they are sprinkled throughout. However, a large clump of white in the middle of other colors tends to create a dead space.

Color also affects our sense of distance and size. Bright colors such as yellow and white tend to jump forward, making things appear closer and bigger. In contrast, red and blue are receding colors. If you want to make your garden look larger than it is, plant trees and shrubs with dark foliage or put blue flowers at the far end. Then grow something yellow up front to accentuate the difference.

The easiest way to create a color-theme garden is to mass-plant one type of flower in one color. For a more sophisticated effect, try combining different types of flowers of the same—or nearly the same—color. For example, plant the daisylike flowers of yellow rudbeckia with *Helenium inula* (sneezeweed), and *Lysimachia punctata* (yellow lysimachia) for a sunny yellow border that offers different textures and forms in a monochromatic scheme. When you combine flowers in this way, it's important to know the hue and intensity of each flower type. Otherwise, you may find yourself with a mixture that clashes. Also, be sure you are mixing plants that bloom at the same time.

Another approach to a color-theme garden is to combine colors that are next to each other on the color wheel. Called harmonizing colors, these blend together easily. An example of this mixture is a border with red, orange, and yellow flowers that are either mixed together or grown in a rainbow pattern in which the composition gradually moves from one color to the next.

Many gardeners enjoy the relaxing effects of pastel colors. If that is your preference, opt for a theme garden in shades of blue, pink, and gray with perhaps a hint of soft yellow to enliven the scene.

When planning any garden with a color theme, keep in mind that you do not have to be a slave to your chosen theme. Your goal is to create a living thing of beauty, not a rigid palette in variations of one color. If you think a splash of blue or pink would be irresistible in your white border, put it in. As Gertrude Jekyll wrote in her book *Color Schemes for the Flower Garden:* "It is a curious thing that people will sometimes spoil some garden project for the sake of a word. For instance a blue garden, for beau-

ty's sake, may be hungering for a group of white lilies, or something of the palest lemon-yellow, but is not allowed to have it because it is called the blue garden, and there must be no other flowers.... Any experienced colorist knows that the blues will be more telling—more purely blue—by the juxtaposition of rightly placed complementary color."

A White Garden

A white garden is ideal for working couples who often aren't home until after dark. Except on the darkest nights, the pale-colored flowers will show up, unlike with deeper colors such as blue and red, which disappear at dusk. There are even a few flowers that remain closed until the cool of the evening, when they open to release a heady fragrance designed to attract night-flying, pollinating insects.

You don't have to have a lot of space for a white garden. Even a small bed, carefully planted with

white-flowering varieties of annuals and perennials, can add aesthetic interest to your garden. With careful planning, it is possible to have something in bloom throughout most of the year. The following are some suggestions for plant choices:

During the spring months, hardy bulbs, which are planted in the fall, can provide the mainstay of the garden. Crocuses, short lived but very early bloomers, are charming in the foreground or cropping up among rocks. Among the white-flowering narcissus are 'Thalia', a single daffodil that is excellent for naturalizing and has long-lasting flowers; paperwhites, sweetly-scented, profuse bloomers that are so hardy they have been known to survive for years in deserted gardens; and 'Mount Hood', which many gardeners consider one of the best white daffodils on the market.

White-flowering azaleas and rhododendrons provide a dramatic burst of blossom in midspring, and the rich green foliage serves as an attractive background for most of the remaining year.

By late spring or early summer, the next series of blooms will appear. A white wisteria trained on a trellis or an arbor creates a spectacular cascade of blossoms. Many gardeners have found that if wisterias

Blue is a restful, soothing color theme for the garden. Here iris and clematis blooms, far left, blend harmoniously while a touch of white astilbe, center, brightens the blue hydrangeas. A splash of yellow, right, can make a blue garden come alive.

are pruned after their first spring bloom, they will flower again in the summer. A climbing white rose, if it is a repeat bloomer, has the added advantage of continuing to flower throughout the summer and fall.

Calla lilies are an excellent choice, as they are easy to grow and produce long-lasting cut flowers. Iris, with their fascinating flower form, are another good addition. Consider less common varieties such as the stately Louisiana and Japanese types.

During the summer months, fill the bed with a wide variety of annuals and perennials. Create a pleasing combination of heights and flower forms by planting the taller plants in back and mixing spiked blooms among the more common, rounded flowers. Annuals and perennials such as cosmos, columbine, zinnias, stock, snapdragons, petunias, phlox, pinks, daisies, begonias, impatiens, balloon flowers *(Platycodon grandiflorus),* and nicotiana all mix well.

Let the harvest moon shine on asters, chrysan-

Plants for a Moonlight Garden

There are hundreds of plants with white flowers. The following list focuses on night-blooming flowers and fragrant white blossoms that add their sweet scent to nighttime enjoyment of the garden. Also included are plants with silver or white variegated foliage that continue the white theme when the flowers are gone.

FLOWERS THAT OPEN AT NIGHT

Datura inoxia (angels' trumpets), grown as annual in cold climates

Ipomoea alba (moonflower), fragrant annual vine

Mirabilis jalapa (four-o'clock), annual

Nymphaea (water lily), some tropical varieties

FRAGRANT WHITE OR CREAM FLOWERS

Brugmansia (angels' trumpets), night-scented flowers, minimum 45°F

Cestrum nocturnum (night jessamine), vine, night-scented flowers, zone 10

Choisya ternata (Mexican orange)

Convallaria majalis (lily of the valley), ground-cover perennial, zones 2-7

Freesia lactea, syn. *F. alba* (freesia), corm, zones 10-11

Gardenia jasminoides (gardenia), zones 8-10

Hedychium coronarium (white ginger lily), zones 9-10

Hosta plantaginea, zones 3-8

Hyacinthus (hyacinth)

Hymenocallis (spider lily), zones vary with species

Jasminum officinal (jasmine), woody climber, zones 9-10

Lathyrus odoratus (sweet pea), annual vine

Lonicera (honeysuckle), zones and flower colors vary with species

Matthiola incana (stock), zones 7-8

Nicotiana sylvestris (tobacco plant), annual or short-lived perennial

Nymphaea (water lily) 'White Delight' and others (tropical)

N. caroliniana 'Nivea' and others (hardy water lily)

Philadelphus (mock orange), zones vary with species

Phlox paniculata 'David' (garden phlox), zones 4-8

Pittosporum tobira (Japanese mock orange), zones 9-10

Polianthes tuberosa (tuberose), temperatures above 59° F

themums, dahlias, and pansies. Pansies are a cool crop that should bloom throughout the winter in all but the coldest regions if they are properly established early in the season and the faded flowers are removed promptly.

Sweet alyssum is a nice choice for the white garden, too. An easy-to-grow ground cover, it is covered with sweet-scented flowers throughout the year. Perhaps this plant's only drawback is that it will self-sow and spread, becoming invasive like a weed. This trait can be a plus, though, when the fragrant white flowers fill any gaps in the garden.

In warm, southern climates, white-flowering camellias can continue the floral interest into the winter months. The sasanqua camellia is sun tolerant, hardy, and the first to bloom in winter. It is followed by the better-known *Camellia japonica*. Varieties vary in their bloom season from very early (October to January) through midseason (January to March) to the late bloomers (March to May).

Primula alpicola (moonlight primrose), zones 4-8

Reseda odorata (mignonette), annual

Rosa (rose), many white-flowering fragrant varieties, zones vary

Stephanotis floribunda (Madagascar jasmine)

SILVER, GRAY AND CREAM VARIEGATED FOLIAGE

Artemisia absinthium (wormwood), zones 4-8

A. arborescens, zones 5-9

A. ludoviciana (western mugwort), zones 4-9

A. stellerana (dusty-miller), zones 3-7

Cornus alba 'Elegantissima' (variegated red-stemmed dogwood), zones 2-8

C. alternifolia 'Argentea' (Pagoda dogwood), zones 4-8

C. controversa 'Variegata' (giant dogwood), zones 6-9

Cotoneaster horizontalis 'Variegatus', zones 6-9

Eryngium variifolium (Moroccan sea holly), zones 5-9

Euonymus fortunei var. *radicans* 'Silver Queen', zones 5-9

Fragaria vesca 'Variegata' (alpine strawberry), zones 5-9

Hedera canariensis 'Gloire de Marengo' (Canary Island ivy), zones 7-10

H. colchica 'Dentata Variegata' (Persian ivy), zones 5-10

H. helix 'Glacier' and other variegated cultivars (English ivy), zones 5-10

Holcus mollis 'Albovariegatus' (ornamental grass), zones 5-9

Hosta albomarginata, zones 3-8

H. fortunei 'Marginata-alba', zones 3-8

H. 'Francee', zones 3-8

Hydrangea macrophylla 'Mariesii Variegata', zones 6-10

Ilex aquifolium 'Ferox Argentea' (English holly), zones 7-9

I. aquifolium 'Silver Milkboy' (English holly), zones 7-9

Lamium maculatum 'Beacon Silver' and 'Silver Pewter' (spotted deadnettle), zones 4-8

Osmanthus heterophyllus 'Latifolius Variegatus' (false holly), zones 7-9

Phalaris arundinacea var. *picta* (ribbon grass), zones 4-9

Philadelphus coronarius 'Variegatus' (mock orange), zones 5-8

Rhamnus alaternus 'Argenteovariegata' (Indian buckthorn), zones 7-9

Saxifraga stolonifera (mother of thousands), zones 6-9

Stachys byzantina (lamb's ears), zones 4-10

Verbascum (mullein), zones vary with species

Vinca major 'Variegata' (periwinkle), zones 7-11

CHAPTER THREE

Defining the Borders of Your Garden Room

I n order to have distinction, a room needs to have defined boundaries. In the garden, those boundaries can take many forms. The obvious approach is to surround each room with a hedge, fence, wall, or trellis. An enclosed garden room is special, but there are many other ways you can distinguish spaces within your garden.

Indoors, a change of level, such as a step down into a sunken living room, indicates a different room. The same is true outside. Even without walls or other barriers, you will feel you've entered a new and distinct space in the garden if you have to step up or down to enter it. You can enhance that impression further by giving the gardens on each level a different look or mood.

A change in paving material, or a switch from hardscape to planted ground cover, also gives the impression of separate garden rooms. For example, even without a partition such as a hedge, flower border, or low fence, a paved patio is perceived as separate from an adjoining lawn. Similarly, a deck or balcony is easily distinguished from the rest of the landscape.

If a path or perennial border bisects a space, it will feel like an integral part of a room. However, if it runs along the edge of the area, it acts as a boundary defining the room's border. As you think about creating different rooms within your garden, be sensitive to the multitude of ways you can make each area feel well defined and separate, and yet part of the whole.

Walls

The English word paradise comes from the old Persian word *pairidaeza*, which means a walled park or pleasure garden. Indeed, by enclosing your garden with a wall, you create a space set apart from the outside world that has the potential to be paradise.

A PERGOLA RUNNING ALONG THE SIDE OF A GARDEN SERVES AS AN ATTRACTIVE BORDER AS WELL AS A PASSAGE FROM ONE GARDEN ROOM TO ANOTHER AND A SHADY PLACE TO SIT.

Because a high wall blocks the surrounding view, the garden is freed from the local setting; no longer tied to its surroundings, it becomes a fantasy space.

In addition, walls give a sense of permanence to a garden and can make a young garden feel old and well established. Since a garden is constantly changing as plants grow and die, the continuity of a wall is reassuring.

The standard materials for walls include brick, stone, and concrete blocks. You can cover concrete block walls with stucco, paint, or other veneers such as stone or brick to make them more attractive. Stone and brick are the classic materials for garden walls because they are derived from the earth and blend comfortably in a variety of garden settings.

The materials used to make a wall (as well as the wall's style) often indicate a particular region of the country, thus adding to a sense of place. Stone walls made from rocks unearthed from the fields each spring are a common feature of the New England landscape. Adobe walls are indigenous to the Southwest, and in the South, brick walls often have a decorative perforated design that allows for cooling air circulation.

Building a Brick Wall on a Budget

Building a brick wall usually requires a sizable investment in both time and money. However, a new

technique introduced by the Brick Institute of America—called pier-and-panel construction— makes it possible to build a brick wall for a fraction of what it would cost using traditional methods.

Normally a straight wall must be thick enough to provide lateral stability, with sufficient strength to resist wind and impact loads. To make the wall structurally sound, you have to build a concrete foundation, or footing, two times thicker than the wall it supports or two-thirds the height of the wall, whichever is greater. In cold climates, the footing must be thick enough to extend below the frost line. The footing runs the entire length of the wall: Digging it, disposing of the dirt, and pouring the concrete represents a significant portion of the cost of construction.

With the pier-and-panel construction technique, the wall can be as narrow as 4 inches (one brick thick), and the panel sections are laid directly on bare earth. Structural support comes from the piers, which are built on standard footings, and from narrow ribbons of galvanized reinforcing wire that run through the layers of mortar in the brick panels and connect to the piers.

A pier-and-panel wall requires about half the number of bricks used to build a standard 8-inch wall, thus significantly reducing the cost of materi-

als. In addition, builders estimate that the time spent on labor is almost cut in half because the footing does not have to be dug. Overall you'll probably save at least 30 percent on the cost of a traditional brick wall.

Building a brick wall without footings goes against everything masons have ever been taught. You're likely to encounter skepticism if you ap-

LEFT: ROSES TRAINED OVER THE OLD BRICK WALL RAISE COLOR TO EYE LEVEL. RIGHT: A WHITE STUCCO WALL MAKES THIS SMALL SUBURBAN GARDEN A PRIVATE HAVEN DESPITE THE PROXIMITY OF NEIGHBORS.

proach a bricklayer with the project. However, this method does work. (For more information and specifications on building a pier-and-panel wall without footings under the panels, contact the Brick Institute of America, 11490 Commerce Park Drive, Reston, Virginia 22091 {web site: www.brickinfo.org} and ask for "Technical Notes on Brick Construction 29A revised, Reissued September 1988.")

Fences

Fences are designed to enclose. Originally they were used as an efficient, relatively inexpensive way of keeping animals in a contained area—or out of one. For example, settlers at Plymouth and Jamestown enclosed their gardens with fences to keep out the pigs, chickens, and other livestock wandering about. As a result, we expect to see a fence that connects to something—either to itself to make an enclosed area, or to a wall or other end point. A fence left floating in the garden with no logical end point is unsettling and ineffective.

Because a fence is an architectural feature, its design should also tie in with the house. A picket fence is charming for a moderately sized, colonial-style home, but looks silly around an opulent house. Wrought-iron fencing suits Victorian architecture, and post-and-rail fences look right in farm country. When you plan for a fence, consider how the style will relate to your home and to other features in the garden.

Sometimes budget must take precedence over all other considerations. In those cases, a chain-link

TOP: DAYLILIES PUSHING UP IN THE NARROW SPACE BETWEEN THIS WROUGHT IRON FENCE AND THE PAVING BRINGS THE GARDEN TO THE STREET WITHOUT LOSING THE SENSE OF BOUNDARY.
RIGHT: PINK COSMOS BRIGHTEN THIS GRAY, WEATHERED SPLIT RAIL FENCE.

fence, however unattractive, may be the most practical option. If you end up getting a chain-link fence or already have one on your property, consider covering it with a dense-growing vine. Ivy is an excellent choice because it will grow in sun or shade and is tolerant of almost any soil. In frost-free climates, bougainvillea, with its vivid-colored flowers borne through the summer and into autumn, makes a dense evergreen curtain that completely hides the unsightly fence underneath. Other good evergreen vines for disguising an ugly fence include cross-vine *(Bignonia capreolata)* and *Clematis armandii.* In cold regions of the country, the selection of vigorously growing vines is greater if you are willing to consider deciduous plants.

Trellises

The Italians first used the art of treillage for their great villa gardens in the 1500s; a century later the Dutch became the masters of the art. André Lenôtre, the great French architect and landscape designer who created Versailles for King Louis XIV, imported Dutch craftsmen to make the trelliswork for the garden at Chantilly in the 1670s.

A trellis is as great an asset in today's gardens at it was 300 years ago. A lattice wall or fence defines

the border of a property or garden room, giving a sense of privacy while also allowing glimpses through the screen. It is perfect for situations where you want a partition but not a solid enclosure. A trellis is like an invisible wall: It's there, but not an overbearing presence. In addition, the shade patterns cast by a trellis are as fascinating and attractive as the trellis itself. In a hot climate with bright sun, the filtered light is especially welcome.

Trellis- or latticework is also a useful tool for improving the appearance of unattractive walls and fences. For example, you can cover a blank wall or fence with an unusual trellis design. You might want to consider arranging the trellis slats to make it look as though there is an arched doorway in the wall. On a house wall, a decorative lattice framework around the windows can create the illusion of lacy shutters. Don't be afraid to paint the latticework an unusual color that ties in with other features in your garden.

Add trelliswork to the top of a fence for extra privacy or to screen an unwanted view without making the fence feel too tall and imposing. Put up a trellis to hide unattractive items such as air condi-

TOP: THIS TRELLIS SCREENS AN UNATTRACTIVE STREET VIEW FOR A PRIVATE PATIO. IT CURVES SLIGHTLY TO GIVE A PLEASING SENSE OF ENCLOSURE. RIGHT: PASTEL GREEN TRELLIS DECORATES AN OTHERWISE PLAIN STUCCO WALL.

tioners or pool equipment, or to screen off utilitarian areas of the garden, such as your compost heap.

Grow vines on the trellis to add to its appeal. Honeysuckle vines are excellent for this purpose. For a long season of flowering interest, choose a mixture of species such as *Lonicera* x *americana*, which produces fragrant yellow blossoms in summer; *L. japonica* 'Halliana', a vigorous vine with pure white flowers that age to yellow; and *L.* x *purpusii* 'Winter Beauty', which produces fragrant white flowers with bright yellow anthers in winter and early spring.

In addition to growing vines up a trellis, you can add color and drama by growing flowering annuals in planters along the top. Attach window boxes to the top of the trellis using brackets designed to affix planters to deck railings, or build planting troughs into the structure itself. Choose annuals, such as geraniums, lobelia, impatiens (for semi shaded areas), ageratum, begonias, and petunias, that will flower generously and continuously throughout the growing season. Plant trailing varieties on the edges so they can cascade down to meet the upward-growing vines.

Hedges

Although it takes patience to wait for them to grow, hedges are a wonderful way to define the borders of your garden rooms. Low-growing hedges are like partitions, dividing the space but allowing a view over the top. A high hedge provides complete privacy.

In addition to adding structure to a design, hedges make wonderful backdrops, showing off perennial borders to perfection and framing pretty garden scenes. They can also be a feature in themselves. Plant a hedge of azaleas and enjoy the spectacular spring flower display. Or choose from a variety of shrubs that produce scented flowers for a heady, fragrant experience.

For security, plant a hedge of shrubs with sharp thorns, such as wintergreen barberry *(Berberis julianae)*, which grows up to 10 feet tall and produces clusters of sweetly scented yellow flowers in late spring. Another good choice is *Pyracantha angustifolia*, which also grows up to 10 feet tall and is covered with small white flowers in midsummer, followed by orange-yellow berries.

For a tapestry effect, combine shrubs—some evergreen, others deciduous—that have leaves with different colors and textures. For example, try mixing barberry, western red cedar *(Thuja plicata)*, golden privet *(Ligustrum vulgare 'Aureum')*, *Osmanthus*, and *Phillyrea*.

A hedge on "stilts" is another intriguing garden concept. Plant small trees such as hornbeam or hawthorn in an even row, and prune the crowns to make an uninterrupted "wall" of foliage on top of the bare trunks.

Selecting the Right Plant for a Hedge

Almost any shrub planted in a row will grow into a hedge. If you want a traditional, pruned hedge with a tailored appearance, opt for shrubs that tolerate shearing well. Plants traditionally used for hedges include yew, boxwood, hornbeam, holly, and privet, all of which grow slowly and need pruning less often.

When considering the many options available, first decide whether you want an evergreen or a deciduous hedge. Although deciduous plants are leaf-

---

Cost-Effective Hedges

It can be very costly to plant a long hedge if you are using large container-grown plants from the nursery. Save money by ordering small, young plants (bare-root is cheapest for deciduous shrubs). In many cases, smaller plants quickly catch up in size to larger ones planted at the same time because they experience less transplant shock.

A DARK GREEN, PRUNED HEDGE IS AN IDEAL BACKGROUND TO SHOW OFF BLOOMING FLOWERS. HERE IT ALSO SCREENS THE VIEW OF THE NEIGHBOR'S HOUSE. IN MOST COMMUNITIES THE HEIGHT REGULATION FOR WALLS AND FENCES DOES NOT APPLY TO HEDGES.

less during the winter months, many offer flowers and berries as well as autumn foliage color. In winter, the network of bare branches adds stark beauty to the landscape.

Next, you need to decide how tall and wide you want the hedge to be. If you're looking for a low barrier to act as a partition between garden rooms, select a low-growing shrub. For example, dwarf boxwood is useful for creating garden parterres because the plant grows slowly (reducing the need for pruning) and tops out at 12 to 18 inches, depending on the variety. Dwarf barberry (*Berberis thunbergii* 'Crimson Pygmy'), another good choice for a low barrier, reaches 24 inches high at maturity. At the other extreme, Leyland cypress (x *Cupressocyparis leylandii*), which can be sheared for a formal hedge or left to grow naturally, can reach 120 feet tall and 15 feet wide. You'll find information on the mature height and width of various plants in most plant encyclopedias.

You also need to consider the growing conditions—for example, the amount of sun the spot gets, whether the area is low-lying and soggy after a heavy rain, and the kind of soil (clay, sand, or loam) you have. Another important variable is the air quality; plants growing along busy roads, for instance, should be tolerant of air pollution. Your hedge will grow more successfully and be more attractive if you choose a plant that is suited to the environment.

Good Plants for Hedges

TREES

Alnus cordata (Italian alder), zones 5-7, fast-growing

Arbutus unedo (strawberry tree), zones 8-9, slow to medium growth rate

Crataegus monogyna (singleseed hawthorn), zones 5-7, slow to medium growth rate

Fagus sylvatica (European beech), zones 4-7, slow to medium growth rate

Ilex aquifolium (English holly), zones 7-9, slow-growing

Olea europaea (olive), zones 9 - 10, slow-growing

Populus x *canadensis* (Canadian poplar), zones 4-9, fast-growing

Prunus lusitanica (Portugal laurel), zones 7-9, medium growth rate

Zelkova serrata (Japanese zelkova), zones 6-8, medium growth rate

J. scopulorum (Rocky Mountain juniper), zones 4-7, medium growth rate

Larix decidua (European larch), zones 3-6, medium to fast growth rate

Picea omorika (Serbian spruce), zones 5-8, slow-growing

Pinus nigra (European black pine), zones 5-8, medium growth rate

P. radiata (Monterey pine), zones 7-9, medium growth rate

Pseudotsuga menziesii (Douglas fir), zones 5-7, medium growth rate

Taxus baccata (English yew), zones 7-8, slow-growing

Thuja plicata (western red cedar), zones 6-8, slow to medium growth rate

Tsuga canadensis (Canada hemlock), zones 4-8, medium growth rate

CONIFERS

Abies grandis (giant fir), zones 5-6, slow to medium growth rate

Cedrus deodara (deodar cedar), zones 7-9, medium growth rate

Cephalotaxus fortunei (Chinese plum yew), zones 6-9, slow-growing

Chamaecyparis lawsoniana (Lawson false cypress), zones 5-9, medium growth rate

x *Cupressocyparis leylandii* (Leyland cypress), zones 6-9, very fast-growing

Juniperus chinensis (Chinese juniper), zones 4-10, slow to medium growth rate

J. communis (common juniper), zones 2-6, slow-growing

SHRUBS

Abelia x *grandiflora* (glossy abelia), zones 6-9, fast-growing

Berberis species (barberry), zones vary, slow to medium growth rate, depending on species

Buxus species (boxwood), zones vary, slow-growing

Camellia species, zones vary, slow-growing

Cotoneaster species, zones vary, slow-growing

Dodonaea viscosa (hop bush), zones 9-10, fast-growing

Duranta erecta (golden dewdrop), zone 10, medium growth rate

Elaeagnus x *ebbingei*, zones 7-10, medium to fast growth rate

E. pungens (silverberry), zones 7-9, very fast-growing

Euonymus species, zones vary, growth rate varies with species

Griselinia littoralis (broadleaf), zones 8-9, fast-growing

Hibiscus species, zones vary, medium growth rate

Ilex cornuta (Chinese holly), zones 7-9, slow-growing

I. crenata (Japanese holly), zones 6-8, slow-growing

I. glabra (inkberry), zones 5-9, slow-growing

Lavandula species (lavender), zones vary, slow-growing

Ligustrum species (privet), zones vary, fast-growing

Lonicera nitida (box honeysuckle), zones 6-9, fast-growing

Osmanthus species, zones vary, slow to medium growth rate

Photinia x *fraseri* (photinia), zones 7-10, medium to fast growth rate

Pittosporum species, zones 9-10, slow-growing

Prunus laurocerasus (English laurel), zones 6-9, medium growth rate

P. lusitanica (Portuguese laurel), zones 7-9, medium growth rate

Pyracantha coccinea (scarlet firethorn), zones 6-10, medium to fast growth rate

Rosmarinus officinalis (rosemary), zones vary, medium growth rate

Tamarix ramosissima (five-stamen tamarisk), zones 2-10, fast-growing

Finally, when you've narrowed down the possibilities, visit a local nursery, and talk with a qualified plantsman to find out which plants would do best in your region and in the specific site you've selected for your hedge.

Planting a Hedge

To make sure the hedge will be straight, place a stake in the ground at each end of the site for the hedge, then run string between the two stakes. If you are making a curved line, stretch a hose on the ground where you want the hedge to be.

Set out the plants along the line. To form a solid hedge, plant them closer together than the normal recommended spacing. For example, *Taxus* x *media* 'Densiformis' is expected to grow to 4 feet tall and to 6 feet wide. If you choose this shrub for your hedge, space the plants no more than 2 feet apart. (Measure from the center of each plant.) For a 50-foot-long hedge, you'll need 25 plants.

For years, gardeners planting trees and shrubs have been advised to dig a hole twice as deep and wide as the rootball and to backfill the large hole with amended soil. Recently, however, researchers have discovered that the roots of trees and shrubs have a difficult time penetrating the native soil if they've been nurtured by an amended mixture. Instead, the roots tend to circle inside the rich planting hole, and eventually the plants become rootbound. Choose plants that are suited to the local soil conditions, and dig your planting holes just large enough to accommodate the rootball. If your soil is heavy clay, plant each tree or shrub so the rootball is about 2 inches above ground level to keep the roots from suffocating if water collects in the planting hole.

Fill each planting hole with water and let it drain away. Remove containerized plants from their pots and loosen the rootball if the roots are tight or encircling the ball. Don't be afraid to cut away the outer layer of roots altogether, if necessary. The surgery will stimulate the roots to produce new feeders that will give the plant a good start.

In the case of balled-and-burlapped plants, remove the burlap completely. Today, many growers wrap the roots in synthetic burlap that looks identical to the old burlap made of natural fibers. However, synthetic burlap won't break down in the soil; if it's left on, eventually the plant will die.

For bare-root plants, create a mound in the bottom of the planting hole and spread the roots over the mound. Make sure the plant is at the same level it was before. You should see soil stains on the trunk indicating the original planting depth.

As you plant, make sure each shrub or tree is centered on the line of the hedge and is the right distance from its neighbors. Check the measurements frequently as you work. One mistake will affect the entire row, and it's easier to make adjustments early on than at the end of the job.

Once you're confident the plant is properly positioned, fill in any gaps around the rootball with soil. Then firmly tamp down the soil around each plant to ensure good contact between the rootball and the soil and to remove any air pockets. Water again, letting the hose run slowly so the water seeps in. Spread a 2- to 4-inch layer of mulch around each plant to reduce moisture evaporation and to suppress weeds. To discourage pests and diseases, be sure to keep the mulch from touching the central trunk or branches of the plants.

Pruning Hedges

Not all hedges have to be sheared into a tight, formal form. Even shrubs such as yew and boxwood that we normally associate with formal, pruned hedges can be left unpruned if you want a casual, billowy look. However, you may still want to do some pruning to encourage bushy growth. In this case, instead of shearing you can hand-trim the shrubs to keep a more natural-looking form. Cut back individual branches to a new growth bud (where you see swelling on the stem), moving along the length of the hedge and across the top of the plants to maintain a balanced shape. This pruning technique is also suitable for large-leaved plants that looked unsightly if they are sheared.

Start pruning and shaping a formal hedge at the beginning of its second season. In late winter before the spring growth begins, cut back the protruding branches by about half. This winter pruning will stimulate vigorous growth once the weather warms up.

You'll need to begin shaping the plants when they're still small. Whatever the final shape, sheared hedges should be slightly wider at the bottom than at the top to allow light to reach all the branches; otherwise, you're likely to end up with leafless gaps along the bottom. Once the hedge is established, you may want to set up a pruning guide to help you cut in an even, straight line. Simply put a post at either end of the hedge and stretch a string between the posts along the hedge's length.

Creative Hedge Training

Instead of training a standard rectangular hedge with a flat top, think about trimming to create extra architectural detail. You can do this by simply allowing sections of the hedge to grow taller at regular intervals, then trimming the longer branches into boxed teeth along the top. If that's too dramatic, consider just training "finial posts" at each end of the hedge.

Another option is to create garden alcoves along the length of a hedge, by planting additional hedges perpendicular to the main one. You might prune the side hedges so they slope downward from the main hedge, making them resemble buttresses supporting the garden "wall" behind.

If you want to allow a glimpse through the hedge to a garden on the other side, think about cutting a window—or a series of windows—in the foliage. You might want square windows to echo the garden room, or arched windows for a Romanesque design. If Gothic is more to your taste, cut the windows so they curve to a point at the top.

A thick hedge is ideal for creating niches within the living wall. Instead of an arbor made of wood or metal, carve one out of the hedge just big enough for a bench or seat to fit inside. Statues, especially white ones that stand out against dark green foliage, look lovely set in niches carved into hedges.

ABOVE: PRUNE A WINDOW IN YOUR HEDGE TO GIVE AN INTRIGUING GLIMPSE INTO ANOTHER PART OF THE GARDEN. FAR RIGHT: PRUNED TO CREATE ARCHITECTURAL "GATE POSTS," THIS LOW HEDGE IS A LOVELY BOUNDARY AROUND THE PERENNIAL GARDEN.

CHAPTER FOUR

Creating the Floor of Your Garden Room

There are a number of ways you can pave or carpet the floor of your garden rooms. For interest and variety, you'll probably want a mixture of paving, grass, and ground covers. Used effectively, each helps create a pleasing design.

Hardscape paving ties the house to its surroundings and provides a clean surface for walking or entertaining. Visually a paved area is set apart from the rest of the garden as a separate garden room. Also, because the surface isn't a plant material, the space works well as a transition from indoor to outdoor rooms.

A well-kept lawn makes a wonderful, verdant carpet, and is ideal if you want a recreational area for games such as croquet, badminton, and volleyball, as well as a place where children can run about and play. A long stretch of green lawn is a restful feature in the garden, easy on the eyes and senses. However, this unabashed horizontal design element also risks being boring. As with all aspects of your garden, plan a lawn carefully so it complements and contrasts with other garden features.

There is a wide choice of plants suitable for ground covers, including ones that tolerate drought, poor soil, and other adverse growing conditions. Once a ground cover is well established so invading weeds cannot take root, it is generally easy to care for—ideal for gardeners who want a tidy look in the garden without a lot of work. In addition, you can introduce a range of color and texture to the garden floor with the right ground cover.

Creative Pavings

Garden rooms with hard surface floors extend the living space of your home. While traditional paving materials include natural stone and brick, many successful designs are created by mixing two or more materials. For example, brick makes a beauti-

A CHECKERBOARD PATTERN COMPRISED OF DIFFERENT COLORED GRAVEL AND LOW-GROWING SUCCULENTS MAKES AN INTRIGUING GARDEN FLOOR. THE GRAVEL SECTIONS ARE SUITABLE FOR WALKING.

ful contrasting edge to a patio made of flagstones or even cast concrete.

Learn about the many different paving possibilities, and choose those that will fit your budget and the style you want for your garden. When working out the cost, keep in mind that while most paved surfaces are expensive to install, they are virtually maintenance-free, with little or no upkeep costs, although some wood needs to be painted periodically with preservative. In the long run, paving generally is much less costly than a lawn or even many ground covers.

CONCRETE ～ Probably least expensive is the old standby: a poured concrete slab. While serviceable, it's pretty bleak looking. For a little extra money you can improve the appearance of a plain slab by tinting the concrete with special pigments before it's poured. Another trick is to incorporate other materials, such as flecks of silica carbide, into the mix. The silica sparkles in the sun like tiny diamonds.

You can create a textured surface by brushing a stiff broom over the concrete before it sets. Another way to make an attractive surface on concrete is called seeded aggregate. While the concrete is still wet, spread pea gravel or another fairly fine material across the top and tamp it into the setting concrete. The result is a finish that looks like a gravel surface, but the gravel won't drift.

Some companies tint the concrete to resemble adobe, and then use a mold or stamp to create a brick or tile-like pattern after its poured. Although the pressed design lacks the color variation and natural irregularity of the materials it's imitating, it is a less-expensive alternative.

TILES ～ Terra-cotta and glazed tiles are beautiful possibilities for garden paving. The mellow terra-cotta color fits well into almost any garden design. Brightly-colored, glazed tiles—which are made in Mediterranean countries such as Spain and Portugal—generally look better in hot climates with intense sunlight, such as Southern California and the Southwest.

If you live in an area that freezes in the winter, be sure you choose tiles that are frost-proof. Tiles durable enough to withstand the stresses of freezing and thawing have been developed by re-fusing pulverized granite. The resulting product is almost diamond-hard. Some of these tiles come in matching indoor and outdoor versions, so continuity can be created between indoor and outdoor spaces. The outdoor version is glazed with a fine silica sand that makes it more slip-resistant when wet.

STONE ～ Stone, with all its natural variations in shape, color, and texture, is an especially beautiful paving in the garden. There are many types of stone suitable for paving. Most people are familiar with flagstone (although that term is a generic expression for any type of stone that has been cut into flat slabs). Specific types of stones that are cut into flagstones for garden use include limestone, sandstone, and slate.

Limestone is a durable stone, although is relatively soft when first quarried. Over time, it hardens as it is exposed to weather. (Keep in mind that it is porous, which makes it less ideal in regions of the country that experience a lot of freezing and thawing in the winter.) Generally cream colored, some varieties are slightly red or yellow with a hint of gray. Some pieces have shells and fossilized animals and plants embedded in the surface.

Sandstone comes in several colors ranging from cream, pink and crimson to greenish brown, cream, and blue-gray. The paler colored stones tend to be stronger, the reddish or brown sandstone is softer and easier to cut.

Slate is used both indoors and outside. Different minerals within the slate affect its color. You'll find black, blue, gray, red, purple, and even green slate. Ribbon slate, which is less expensive than pieces that are uniform in color, is striped with two colors. Durable and weather resistant, slate is an excellent paving material. It is brittle, however, and tends to break off in layers.

GRAVEL, SAND, AND CHIPPED STONE ⌁
Gravel is a versatile, relatively inexpensive material that looks equally at home in formal and informal, east coast and west coast settings. In the Southwest, where drought is a major factor in gardening, mulches of chipped marble, volcanic stone, gravel, and other types of rock are useful alternatives to water-hungry lawns.

Gravel paths and patios that have to hold up under a lot of traffic should be properly laid with an un-

AGGREGATE CONCRETE

CRAZY QUILT STONE SLABS

SPANISH TILE

FLAGSTONE

der surface of crushed stone or rubble, followed by a clay binder and the gravel. Otherwise, you can spread the gravel directly onto the ground. To minimize weeds, lay down vinyl sheeting or thick plastic over the ground before you spread the stone.

Avoid putting gravel at the bottom of any slope because the particles of soil running off the slope will muddy the stone. You'll also have a neater garden if you contain gravel with raised edges around the perimeter

Raked sand gardens, made from decomposed gravel, embody the Japanese minimalist style of gardening. Originally sand was spread on the ground to keep feet from getting muddy. Eventually Zen masters began creating patterns in the sand to represent philosophical themes. The patterns are made with wooden rakes especially designed for that purpose.

COBBLES ॐ Cobbles are smooth, naturally rounded stones. The smaller ones found on beaches are created by being tossed about in the waves and dragged along the shoreline. Small cobbles can be laid so the flattest side faces the top, or set on edge to create serrated rows of narrow ridges. In either case, set the cobbles in mortar, and pack them together as

GRAVEL AND HEAT-LOVING PLANTS

TRADITIONAL BRICK

PEBBLE MOSAIC

WOOD DECKING

tightly as possible so the mortar doesn't show.

Although cobblestones are uncomfortable to walk upon, they are extremely decorative, especially when they are set in pretty patterns. Use them in conjunction with other pavings that are easier on the feet. For example, you might use a mosaic of cobblestones as the central motif in the middle of a patio, or as an artistic element to draw the eye toward a particular area of the patio. You also might combine small areas of cobbles within an expanse of smoother paving material: You'll add interest with the diverse textures and materials, while also minimizing the difficulty of walking on a completely uneven surface.

Loose cobbles spread on the ground is another attractive way of paving the garden floor: Japanese gardens often feature pebble "shores" along the edges of ponds or "rivers" made of stone, laid to look like as if it's flowing through the garden. Another Japanese device is creating designs, such as an interlocking yin and yang motif, out of different colored stones.

BRICK ᔭ Brick is a popular, and varied, paving material. If you're making a brick patio or walkway, be sure to specify that you want paving bricks. They are baked longer than other types of bricks to reduce the amount of water they'll absorb. Their nonabsorbant surface is essential, especially in areas of heavy traffic and in regions that experience winter freezing and thawing.

We often refer to the color "brick red," but bricks come in a wide range of colors. There is a great deal of variation within the red color range for bricks from rust to burgundy. In addition you can find bricks in various shades of yellow and dark gray.

You can either set bricks on a concrete foundation and join them with mortar, or lay them dry on a foundation comprised of a 2-inch layer of gravel or rubble topped with a 1-inch layer of dry builder's sand or mortar. Both methods are attractive; garden paths and pavings laid without mortar have a more classic, traditional look to them.

WOOD ᔭ Wooden paving, traditionally used for decks and paths that traverse boggy parts of the garden, blend beautifully in most garden settings. Choose naturally rot-resistant wood, such as red cypress, cedar and redwood, or pressure-treated lumber, which should last approximately 20 years.

You can have fun designing different patterns for a wooden surface. For example, in addition to simply laying the boards parallel or perpendicular to the deck in a running pattern, you can lay them at angles to create a herringbone design, make a series of concentric squares, a V-shape, or a parquet pattern with alternating squares of boards running parallel and perpendicular to the edge.

Other types of wood for garden floors include shredded hardwood bark, which is an attractive mulch that gives a finished look to garden beds and paths. In addition, it helps maintain moisture in the soil, keeps down weeds, and breaks down to add valuable nutrients and organic material to the soil. To look its best, bark mulch should be replaced at least once a year. Wood nuggets, which are broken into larger pieces than the shredded material, break down much more slowly. A thick covering should last several years.

Creating a Garden between Paving Squares

Add color to an expanse of paving stones or bricks with plants growing in especially created spaces. If the paving is laid with large gaps, such as 2 inches or more between blocks, you can plant in the spaces between. The other alternative is to remove the occasional paver and plant in the newly created planter.

If the soil is poor quality and you plan to plant between pavers, you'll want to improve the ground before you lay the paving. Otherwise you'll have a huge job removing stones or bricks next to the cracks so you have room to amend the soil. In situations where you are removing an area of paving to make a planter, you can easily dig out poor quality soil and replenish it with rich loam and organic materials.

With a little hard work, it is possible to remove pavers that are cemented in place in order to make a planting hole. Using a heavy-duty chisel and a hammer, chip away the cement around each paver or a connected group of pavers, and then lever them out with a crowbar. Remove any rubble or cement under the pavers, refill the hole with good quality soil, and plant.

Choose plants that are suited to the situation. The soil will remain cool and moist under the pavers because there is little evaporation. On the other

CREEPING THYMES AND OTHER LOW-GROWING, SPREADING PLANTS SPROUT BETWEEN THE PAVING STONES, SOFTENING THE HARD EDGES AND ADDING INTEREST TO THE STRAIGHT PATH.

hand, the paved surface will absorb heat, making it a hot spot if the area is sunny. Look for plants that will stay compact and low to the ground and low-growing spreaders that will spill onto the paving, softening the edges.

Once you've planted the spaces, cover the remaining exposed soil with pea gravel or another finely crushed stone. This will give your planting a finished look and keep soil from washing onto the paving.

Good Plants to Go between Pavings

Low, mound-forming plants and compact, spreading plants are ideal to grow between pavings. For an added bonus, choose aromatic plants such as thyme, chamomile, and rosemary that release their scent in the hot sun or when crushed underfoot.

Acaena (New Zealand burr), zones vary

Alchemilla mollis (lady's-mantle), zones 4-8

Antirrhinum, dwarf varieties (snapdragon), usually grown as annual

Arabis caucasica (wall rock cress), zones 4-8

Armeria juniperifolia (miniature thrift), zones 5-7

A. maritima (sea thrift), zones 3-9

Calendula officinalis (pot marigold), annual

Chamaemelum nobile 'Treneague' (chamomile), zones 6-9

Cistus (rock rose), zones 8 or 9-10, depending on variety

Corydalis lutea (yellow corydalis), zones 5-8

Cymbalaria muralis (ivy-leaved toadflax), zones 4-8

Dianthus (pinks), zones vary

Diascia, zones 8-9

Erica (heather, heath), zones vary

Erinus alpinus (alpine liverwort), zones 4-7

Helianthemum (rock rose), zones 6-8

Iberis (candytuft), zones vary

Juniperus horizontalis (creeping juniper), zones 3-10

J. procumbens (Bonin Island juniper), zones 5-9

Lobularia maritima (sweet alyssum), annual

Mazus reptans, zones 5-8

Phlox subulata (moss pink), zones 4-9

Rosmarinus (rosemary), zones vary

Sedum, zones vary

Sempervivum (hens and chicks, houseleeks), zones vary

Thymus herba-barona (caraway thyme), zones 4-10

T. serpyllum (mother of thyme), zones 4-9

Tropaeolum (nasturtium)

Veronica prostrata (prostrate speedwell), zones 4-7

Viola (pansy, Johnny-jump-up)

Verdant Lawns

Lawns are usually the heart of American gardens, but they often lack soul. To make a lawn special, it needs to be seen in contrast to other features. In most cases, a garden that is almost exclusively grass is boring.

Rather than using a large lawn area as a "default" planting, plan your garden so your lawn can

---

The Secrets to Success for a Healthy Lawn

It is possible to have a healthy, weed-free lawn without constantly using chemicals. Like many diseases, weeds are opportunistic organisms that tend to invade a weak lawn that doesn't have the strength to compete. If you provide your lawn with a good environment, your trouble will be rewarded with a grass that flourishes without an excess of expensive fertilizers and chemicals, and the weeds will never have a chance to gain a foothold.

GOOD SOIL

Good quality soil is the basis of a healthy lawn. You may get seeds to germinate and struggle along in heavy clay or nutrient-starved sand, but for really vigorous growth you need to provide a humus-rich environment.

If you are starting a lawn from scratch, have a professional laboratory analyze soil samples for you. You'll get a report outlining the soil contents and all the amendments you'll need, as well as how much of each, to bring the soil up to a good standard for grass. Spread the recommended nutrients and organic amendments (well-rotted manure, peat moss, and compost are all good for soil texture) over the ground and rototill in the material to a depth of at least 4 to 6 inches.

You can either completely renovate an established lawn or gradually improve the soil by fertilizing as a top dressing with organic feed such as manure and seaweed that helps improve the structure of the soil. Although generally more expensive than chemical fertilizers, these organic materials supply a steady source of nutrients to the lawn over a long period as well as improving the soil. They are an excellent investment.

RIGHT GRASS IN THE RIGHT PLACE

There are about 40 varieties of grass for home gardens. These are divided into warm-season grasses that do best in the warmer parts of the country (zones 5-11, depending on the variety) and cool-season grasses that grow well in zones 1-6. Within those two groups are grasses suited to different situations. Some are sturdy types that can withstand a lot of foot traffic, others are tolerant of salt spray, or other difficult situations. In addition, in the past decade researchers have made enormous strides in developing grass hybrids that are bred for better long-term performance, disease resistance, deeper roots, and general attractive appearance. Before you purchase seed or sod, find out what grass variety or mixture will best suit your climate, growing conditions, and family needs.

Grass is a sun-loving plant that needs good air circulation. While there are a few grass varieties, such as fine fescue, St. Augustine, and bahia grass, that will tolerate some shade, most will languish if they don't get enough light. In addition, shady spots are more humid than sunny ones and generally have less air circulation. These factors enhance the potential for lawn disease.

For a healthy, vigorous lawn, you need to choose a sunny, open spot in your yard. If you're determined to grow grass in the shade, choose a disease-resistant, shade-tolerant variety that is well suited to your region.

play a key design role. Make it an emerald green gem set among other plantings. Use a restful grassy carpet next to a busy border of multicolored flowers, or as a horizontal foil to vertical elements such as hedges, walls, or trellises. Planted in a special context, the lawn becomes a valuable garden feature. On the practical side, it's much easier (and cost efficient) to keep a small lawn in peak condition than to

DEEP WATERING

To encourage a deep root system that will be more resistant to drought and other problems, water your lawn as deeply and infrequently as possible. Ideally, the water should penetrate the soil at least 6 to 12 inches every time you water, which amounts to approximately 1 to $1^1/_2$ inches of water. One inch of water will penetrate about 12 inches in sandy soil, 7 inches in loam, and 4 to 5 inches in clay. To determine how much water you are delivering with your sprinkler system, place containers around the sprinkled area and notice how long it takes for the water to collect. You'll probably find that some containers will fill faster than others.

Different soils absorb water at different rates. Water disappears into sandy soil almost immediately. Heavy clay absorbs water very slowly, sometimes as little as one-tenth of an inch per hour. If you notice runoff when you water, stop the sprinklers and allow the existing water to soak in before you begin watering again. In cases of extreme clay, you may need to water very slowly for as long as five hours. You can also water, turn off the sprinklers for 10 minutes, wait an hour, and then water again, repeating the cycle until the soil has absorbed the correct amount of water. Sprinklers set on an automatic timer are a great boon if you need to turn them on and off repeatedly to avoid runoff.

DON'T OVERFEED

An overfed lawn will grow too quickly. Fast-growing lawns increase the lawn's susceptibility to pests and diseases because the grass tends to produce lush leaf growth at the expense of developing strong roots. The ideal for a healthy lawn and your budget is to use the minimum amount of fertilizer necessary to keep the grass looking lush and green.

The best way to fertilize a lawn is with a slow-release nitrogen such as sulfur-coated urea, urea formaldehyde, I.B.D.U, natural organic fertilizers such as Milorganite, kelp products such as seaweed ex-tract, and resin-coated urea. Although these are generally more expensive to purchase than fast-release nitrogen fertilizers, they last longer and need to be applied less frequently. As a rule, lawns fed with a slow-release form of nitrogen will have better color, thickness, and reduced leaf growth than lawns treated with quick-release nitrogen.

Grass clippings are good for the lawn. They can provide up to 25 percent of the required nutrients, and when they decompose they add organic material to the soil and encourage the presence of earthworms that aerate the soil. If you mow properly *(see below)* so you aren't removing too much grass at a time, the clippings will not clump and cause thatch. Rather than going to the extra work of collecting and disposing of the clippings, do your lawn a favor and leave them in place.

PROPER MOWING

It's tempting to mow grass short so it looks tidier and doesn't need to be mowed again so soon. This is a bad policy. Grass that is shorn too close is more likely to succumb to stresses caused by drought, insect injury, foot traffic, or too little sun. The frequency of mowing and the ideal length of grass depends on the type of grass you have and other environmental conditions; as a general rule you should never remove more than one-third of the leaf surface each time you mow. The ideal mowing height varies with different types of grass. Bermuda and centipede grass are best kept at $1^1/_2$ inches; bluegrass, perennial ryegrass, buffalograss, fine fescue, St. Augustine, and tall fescue all do well at 2 inches. Zoysia should be kept at 1 to 2 inches.

You'll reduce the chance of disease and improve the appearance of your lawn if your mower blades are sharp. Dull blades tear the grass, rather than making a clean cut. Those ragged edges, which turn brown, giving an unattractive color to the lawn, have more surface area to take in disease.

try to maintain grass that covers thousands of square feet.

In the spring you can dress up your lawn with flowering bulbs. Daffodils and crocus are sturdy bulbs that can push up through turf to add a season of floral color early in the year. A disadvantage of growing bulbs in the lawn is the bulb foliage should be allowed to die back undisturbed after the flowers have faded. Otherwise you'll weaken the bulbs, sacrificing blooms in subsequent years. As a result, the grass where bulbs are planted shouldn't be mown for about six weeks after the bulbs bloom. Two solu-

tions are to plant bulbs in the lawn in a "wild" area of the garden, perhaps some distance from the house, where the cultivated landscape blends seamlessly with undeveloped land beyond. A section of unmown lawn will look natural, and you can tidy up the area later. Alternatively, you can plant the daffodils in the grass near the house where you can easily see them, and accept that the patches of lawn where the daffodils grew may be a little scruffy looking for a few weeks after they flower. To minimize the problem, choose bulbs that bloom very early in the season: They'll be further along in their

SET IN AN ENCIRCLING FRAME OF BLOOMING BULBS AND PERENNIALS, THIS LAWN IS AN EMERALD GEM IN A BEAUTIFUL SETTING.

cycle above ground by the time the lawn is ready for its first shearing in spring.

Ground Covers for Leafy Floors

There are hundreds of possibile ground covers for your garden. In fact, you can classify almost any plant that covers the ground so you see little or no earth as a ground cover. Generally, however, a ground cover is a spreading plant that grows no taller than two feet.

Ground covers are a great option in difficult areas such as steep slopes, deep shade, boggy areas, or extremely dry spots.

On steep slopes, ground-cover roots grip the soil, stopping erosion. Since most ground covers don't require mowing, you're saved negotiating a lawn mower over difficult terrain. Choose plants, such as daylilies for sunny slopes or hostas for shady ones, that require little or no care once they're established. For longer flower interest, plant bulbs as well. The newly sprouting daylily or hosta foliage will hide the unsightly bulb foliage as it dies back. Other good possibilities for slopes include woolly yarrow, ajuga, crown vetch, winter creeper, St.-John's-wort, creeping juniper, rugosa roses, and periwinkle.

Deep shade is a difficult area to plant because it's often very dry as well. Good ground covers in that

situation include ivy (most varieties will tolerate both full sun as well as full shade), pachysandra, periwinkle, and epimedium. See the plant list on page 58 for other good ground covers for shady locations.

Many ground covers are drought tolerant, making them an important part of garden design in regions of the country that experience single digit inches of rain per year. Succulents, such as hardy iceplant *(Delosperma cooperi),* sedum, and sempervivum and gray-leafed plants such as lamb's ears are all very drought tolerant.

In boggy soil ground covers adapted to that environment help soak up the water. Many ferns, primroses, creeping Jenny *(Lysimachia nummula-*

BLUE WILD SWEET WILLIAM (*Phlox divaricata*) AND FOAMFLOWER (*Tiarella cordifolia*) COMBINE FOR A BEAUTIFUL WOODLAND GROUND COVER DISPLAY.

Good Ground Covers

For Shade

Ajuga reptans (bugleweed), zones 3-8, full sun to partial shade

Alchemilla mollis (lady's-mantle), zones 4-8, full sun to partial shade

Asarum caudatum (British Columbia wild ginger), zones 6-8, partial shade

Aspidistra elatior (cast-iron plant), zones 7-10, full shade

Bergenia cordifolia (heartleaf bergenia), zones 3-8, partial shade

Brunnera macrophylla (Siberian bugloss), zones 4-10, partial shade

Ceratostigma plumbaginoides (leadwort), zones 5-9, full sun to partial shade

Chrysogonum virginianum (green-and-gold), zones 5-8, partial shade in North, full shade in South

Clivia miniata (Kaffir lily), zones 9-10, partial shade

Convallaria majalis (lily of the valley), zones 4-9, partial to full shade

Cornus canadensis (bunchberry), zones 2-7, partial shade

Duchesnea indica (Indian strawberry), zones 4-9, full sun to partial shade

Epimedium species, zones 5-9, partial to full shade

Euphorbia amygdaloides var. *robbiae* (wood spurge), zones 7-9, partial shade

Galax urceolata (wandflower), zones -8, full shade

Galium odoratum (sweet woodruff), zones 3-8, full shade

Geranium macrorrhizum (bigroot cranesbill), zones 4-8, full sun to partial shade

Hedera species (ivy), zones 5-9, partial to full shade

Hemerocallis fulva (tawny daylily), zones 2-9, full sun to partial shade

Hosta species and cultivars (plantain lily), zones vary with variety, partial to full shade

Iris cristata (crested iris), zones 4-9, partial shade

Lamium galeobdolon 'Variegatum', zones 4-9, partial to full shade

L. maculatum (spotted deadnettle), zones 4-8, partial to full shade

Liriope spicata (creeping lilyturf), zones 5-10, full sun to full shade

Lysimachia nummularia (creeping Jenny), zones 4-8, full sun in North, full shade in South

Mazus reptans, zones 5-8, full sun to partial shade

Microbiota decussata (Siberian carpet cypress), zones 2-8, sun or shade

Pachysandra terminalis (Japanese spurge), zones 4-8, partial to full shade

Paxistima canbyi (cliff green), zones 5-8, partial shade

Pellionia repens (trailing watermelon begonia), zone 10-11, partial shade

Phlox divaricata (wild sweet William), zones 4-8, partial shade

P. stolonifera (creeping phlox), zones 4-8, partial to full shade

Pulmonaria species (lungwort), zones vary with variety, partial to full shade

Rubus calycinoides (bramble), zones 6-9, full sun to partial shade

Saxifraga stolonifera (strawberry geranium), zones 6-8, partial shade

S. x urbium (London pride), zones 5-8, partial shade

Soleirolia soleirolii (baby's tears), zones 9-11, partial shade

Tiarella cordifolia (foamflower), zones 5-9, partial shade

Vinca minor (periwinkle), zones 4-8, light to moderately heavy shade

Achillea tomentosa (woolly yarrow), zones 3-7	
Arabis caucasica (wall rock cress), zones 4-8	
Aubrieta species, zones 5-7	
Aurinia saxatilis (basket-of-gold), zones 4-7	
Calluna vulgaris (Scotch heather), zones 5-7	
Carpobrotus chilensis (ice plant), zones 10-11	
C. edulis (Hottentot fig), zones 10-11	
Centaurea montana (mountain bluet), zones 3-8	
Cerastium tomentosum (snow-in-summer), zones 4-7	
Chamaemelum nobile (Roman chamomile), zones 3-8	
Cotoneaster horizontalis (rockspray cotoneaster), zones 5-8	
Delosperma cooperi (hardy ice plant), zones 7-10	
Dianthus gratianopolitanus (cheddar pink), zones 5-8	
Euphorbia polychroma (cushion spurge), zones 5-9	
Geranium sanguineum (blood-red cranesbill), zones 4-8	
Iberis sempervirens (perennial candytuft), zones 5-9	
Juniperus communis 'Prostrata' (juniper), zones 3-9	
J. conferta (shore juniper), zones 6-9	
J. horizontalis (creeping juniper), zones 3-10	
J. procumbens 'Nana' (Japanese garden juniper), zones 5-9	
J. sabina var. *tamariscifolia* (Savin juniper), zones 4-7	
Lantana montevidensis (trailing lantana), zones 9-11	
Lithodora diffusa, zones 6-8	
Nepeta mussinii (Persian catmint), zones 3-8	
Phlox subulata (moss pink), zones 4-9	
Sagina subulata (pearlwort), zones 5-7	
Stachys byzantina (lamb's ears), zones 4-10	
Thymus herba-barona (caraway thyme), zones 4-10	
T. praecox ssp. *arcticus* (creeping thyme), zones 5-10	
Veronica prostrata (prostrate speedwell), zones 4-7	

ria), and hostas (which also thrive in very dry conditions) are just a few of the plants that do well in moist conditions.

Once established, ground covers usually require less maintenance than lawns or flower borders; however it is important to be diligent about weeding until the plant cover is dense enough to block out weeds on its own. Otherwise the weeds will take hold, go to seed, and create an unsightly mess that becomes more difficult to control as time passes. Depending on how closely you plant and how quickly your plants grow, you may need to weed regularly for at least the first year or two.

There is a wealth of effects you can create with ground covers. Combine swaths or swirls of plants with different foliage and textures to create a tapestry effect. Choose plants that grow with equal vigor so you don't find one plant dominating the scene at the expense of the slow-growing specimen. Good combinations include foamflower *(Tiarella cordifolia)* and creeping phlox *(Phlox stolonifera),* English ivy and pachysandra, or a mixture of creeping thymes.

You might choose a ground cover such as pachysandra or ivy because its dark green color makes a restful background in your garden, or you might choose a flowering or berry-bearing plant to be a stunning focal point.

For the best success, choose ground covers that are suited to the soil and light conditions, local climate, and amount of moisture available in the specific spot where you plan to put them. The prettiest gardens are ones where the plants look healthy and happy, and plants that are growing in conditions that suit them will look better, grow faster, and be less work to maintain.

CHAPTER FIVE

Thresholds & Doorways

The entrance to a garden, whether marked by a gate or a simple opening, is both a physical and psychological gateway. Ideally a garden entrance should set the mood for the garden, hinting at the charms that lie beyond and beckoning the visitor to enter; it marks the beginning of the garden experience. Your goal is to create a welcoming entrance that makes people feel compelled to come into the garden.

Garden Gates

The opening in a wall or hedge is as important as the structure itself: It suggests other worlds and welcome surprises. If you install a gate into the opening, you add to the sense of suspense and anticipation. A gate can convey many messages. For example, it can exclude, entice or invite.

A tall, solid gate, especially one equipped with a lock, provides privacy and security. People cannot see into the garden, and the messge is clearly "keep out," even without a sign. Those who are allowed access feel privileged. In the classic children's novel *The Secret Garden*, it was the garden sequestered behind a high wall and a hidden, locked gate that enthralled the children and eventually worked its healing magic in their lives.

A privacy gate is a good choice if you live on a busy street or if you simply want the security. Choose a style that complements your house, and make it a special architectural feature. For example, if the gate will be set into a wooden stockade fence, one option is to continue the same pattern on the gate so that it blends seamlessly into the surroundings. But if you do that, the gate will be a nonentity and disguise the fact that there's a garden beyond. Instead, you can make the gate stand out by setting

THE ARCHED OPENING IN THIS STONE WALL IS ENHANCED BY A SIMPLE WROUGHT-IRON GATE WITH A VINING TENDRIL PATTERN. THROUGH THE GATE IS A PARTIAL VIEW OF THE GARDEN, A FORETASTE OF THE PLEASURES TO COME.

the gate boards at an angle or in a herringbone pattern. Consider painting the gate a color that matches the trim on your house, or a different color altogether. That way, the gate will not only provide privacy but also the beginning of a special experience for those lucky enough to be invited inside.

A gate that entices is mostly solid but has open areas that allow glimpses into the garden. A lattice gate, or one made of wrought iron, offers pretty patterns as well as an easy view into the garden. Even more enticing is a tall wooden gate with a small window cut into the upper portion. If you set a decorative, open metalwork design into the window, people will be encouraged to try to glimpse as much of the garden as possible from different angles. The Japanese moon gate, with its circular hole cut in the upper half, is another variation on this idea. You can also create a moon opening by designing the gate so that the top edge is cut in a concave curve, with a matching curve that rises up from the gate posts and arcs across the top of the gate.

With a Dutch gate, you can either allow views into the garden or enjoy complete privacy. The doors are cut in two horizontally across the middle: You can bolt the two halves together so the door swings as one unit, or unlatch them so the top section opens while the bottom remains closed.

A garden gate doesn't have to lead into a garden. For the sake of symmetry or to create the impression that there are additional garden rooms, you may decide to add a gate in a fence, hedge, or garden wall even though the gate leads nowhere. If the ad-

THIS GATE, WITH ITS LATCH AND LOCK, PROVIDES SECURITY, BUT ALSO ALLOWS ENTICING GLIMPSES INTO THE GARDEN. THE WHITE ARBOR OVER THE GATE ADDS A SENSE OF IMPORTANCE TO THIS THRESHOLD.

joining land is undeveloped fields or woodland, choose a gate with a see-through design so you can enjoy the view. There's no harm in creating the illusion that your property is much larger than it actually is, and for the price of a gate you can add imaginary acres to your land.

In addition to placing gates along the garden's perimeter, you may want to consider siting gates within the garden. If you have a separate garden room defined by a wall, hedge, or fence, then a gate is an obvious accessory, but there are other suitable spots for garden gates as well.

Take the case of a patio and lawn, for example. Although the two different surfaces create the impression of two separate garden rooms or spaces, all of those uninterrupted horizontal lines can be visually monotonous. You can make the patio feel more intimate and separate from the garden by putting up a picket fence or planting a low hedge around the perimeter. Another option is to construct a low wall that can double as seating. In addition to defining the space, a border provides a much-needed vertical element to the design. Leave an opening in the wall or hedge so you can move easily from one space to the other, and put in a gate to accentuate the gap. Choose a gate that is exceptionally pretty or unusu-

al so it is a valued focal point and an important feature of the patio.

Gate Designs and Colors

While gates are generally made out of either wood or iron, the designs are virtually unlimited. For example, iron can be cast to make gates with ornate, heavy designs, and wrought iron lends itself to intricate patterns and motifs.

Wooden gate designs are just as varied. Even a

TOP: THE CAREFULLY PRUNED BOXWOOD HEDGE APPEARS TO POINT THE WAY INTO THIS CHARMING SEASIDE GARDEN ROOM. RIGHT: THE PAIR OF WHITE FLOWERING SHRUBS FLANKING THIS GATE HELP INTEGRATE IT INTO THE LANDSCAPE.

simple gate made out of pickets can have any number of finial motifs—including acorn, arrow points, Gothic points, and rounded ornamentation—at the top of each paling. Within the rectangular frame of the gate, creative craftsmen can devise trellis patterns, angled Chippendale fretwork, sunbursts, concentric rectangles, spider's-web networks, or a host of other creative designs.

The supporting posts for gates are typically made of stone, brick, wood, or iron. You can mix and match all of these materials to create unusual and compelling designs.

You'll also need to decide on a color for your garden gate. Wooden slatted gates are pretty if the natural wood is left to weather to a silvery gray. Alternatively, you can unify the house and garden if you paint the wooden gate the same color as the front door, or match the wooden trim on the house.

In the case of a white picket fence, you might paint the gate white to create a continuous pattern, or highlight the gate by painting it a contrasting color. Colors typically used with Chinese Chippendale designs include cinnabar red, antique yellow, and pale blue-green.

Before you settle on a color for a garden gate, look at the scene behind it. If the background is dark green shrubbery or a shady area, choose a light color that will stand out in relief. Otherwise, the ornamental features of the gate will be lost in the darkness. If there is pale foliage or sky behind the gate, choose a dark color—such as black, charcoal gray, or dark blue—that will show up against the light background.

Before you make a major investment in garden gates, do a little research. Take time to look at gates, and think about what it is that makes a particular gate successful. In addition to gates in local gardens, study pictures of gates in magazines and books. If you've done your homework, ultimately the challenge will be to narrow all of the options down to one or two of your favorites.

SUNLIGHT CATCHES THE CURLICUE DESIGN OF THIS WROUGHT-IRON GATE. WROUGHT-IRON IS AVAILABLE IN A VARIETY OF DELICATE PATTERNS.

Alternatives to Gates

The transition from the outside world to the garden or from one garden room to another doesn't have to be marked by a gate.

An arbor—for example, one laden with flowering vines—makes a compelling entrance to a garden room, especially a cottage garden filled to the brim with old-fashioned flowers or an herb garden laid out in a pleasing, geometric pattern. The arbor frames the view like a picture window and adds a satisfying vertical element to the design. In addition, it lends an air of importance to the scene. When we walk underneath arches to pass from one space to another, the journey seems to take on more significance.

You'll add to this sense of importance if you set a gate into the arbor. Choose a gate that is in keeping with the arbor design. A picket gate is ideal for a lattice arbor; wrought or cast iron mixes well with a metal arch; and a gate fashioned out of wooden

THE SQUARE GRID PATTERN IN THIS WOODEN GATE ECHOES THE CUT-OUT DESIGN IN THE STUCCO WALL. THE MUSTARD YELLOW COLOR ADDS TO THE INTEREST, MAKING THE GATE STAND OUT AS A SPECIAL GARDEN FEATURE.

planks would suit an arbor made from untreated wooden beams.

As with a gate, you can position an arbor to make your garden look larger than it actually is. For example, try placing an arbor at the far end of your garden on the property boundary; from a distance, it will look like the opening to another garden room. If you place it along each side and facing each other, the arbor will double as a peaceful, shady retreat where you can go alone or with a friend.

An avenue of trees or shrubs is a dramatic way to enter a new garden space. Instead of going through a doorway, visitors are taken down a long corridor. In this case, moving from one area to another becomes an experience in itself. If you have a large property, you can create openings along the length of the avenue, with paths leading to additional garden rooms.

Sometimes simplicity is the best solution in a garden. Instead of gates and arches, you may decide to simply leave a gap in the hedge or wall. To make this simple transition from one garden room to another a little more special, flank the opening with a pair of urns, statues, obelisks, or columns. To raise the urns to eye level, you can create inexpensive plinths by stacking clay flowerpots turned bottom side up.

MADE BY NAILING SMALL, STRAIGHT TREE OR SHRUB BRANCHES TO HORIZONTAL SUPPORTS, THIS SIMPLE GATE WITH ITS GOTHIC ARCH FITS IN PERFECTLY WITH THE RUSTIC, ROSE-COVERED TRELLIS.

Create an Arched Opening in a Hedge

An arched passage through a hedge can frame a view, create a vista, or simply provide visitors with the special experience of passing under an arch to another space in the garden. It's easy to create an arched opening in a hedge; the most difficult part is waiting for the plants to grow so that the branches can be interlaced—a technique called pleaching.

When you plant your hedge, leave a gap wide enough for a path. If the hedge already exists and you want to make an opening, remove one or two of the plants. Prune the shrubs regularly on the sides to keep the opening clear, but leave the top unpruned to encourage the plants to grow taller. Since the standard height of a doorway in a home is a little under 7 feet, that's probably the minimum height you want for your opening. That means the shrubs need to be even taller, since the branches are eventually pulled together toward the center of the opening to form the arch.

Once the branches on either side of the opening have grown tall enough, bend them over so they connect, and tie them together using string or wire. As the soft, supple branches you're training mature, they'll harden so that eventually they will maintain their shape without the ties. In the meantime, check the ties every few months to make sure they aren't too tight, and adjust or replace them, if necessary.

In the beginning, you'll have a skinny arch above the opening, but over the next few seasons the pleached branches will continue to send up vertical shoots. Eventually you should have a pleasingly solid "lintel" above the doorway.

If you have a good eye and a steady hand, you can prune the arch freehand. Otherwise, install a metal arch inside the opening to use as a pruning guide. You can purchase garden arches through mail-order catalogs; however, they tend to be quite expensive. Since the metal insert arch is not meant for decorative purposes, you might want to make

your own. See Chapter 9, pages 104-105, for information on making an inexpensive arch with rebar.

CHAPTER SIX

Garden Paths

Paths do more than provide a passageway through a garden: They are a strong visual element and contribute significantly to the garden's structure. Therefore, you can use paths to create all sorts of pleasing effects. For example, a path can make a small garden feel much larger than it actually is.

To enlarge a small space visually, run a path straight from the house to the end of the garden. The line of the path will draw the eye to the end, making the distance seem greater than it actually is. To further enhance the illusion, make the path increasingly narrower as it moves away from the house and plant small trees or shrubs on both sides of the path at the end. The visual size of the garden will increase before your eyes, especially if the plants' foliage is a dark color that appears to recede. If the path is made of brick, lay the brick in a running-bond pattern that draws the eye into the distance. And if you cut the bricks at the far end slightly shorter than the standard length, because they are small, they'll look even farther away.

Another device you can use to increase the sense of distance is to position ornaments—such as a series of statues or urns—along the path, leaving less space between each ornament as the path moves toward the far end. If you cannot afford that many ornaments, plant pairs of shrubs along the pathway, gradually decreasing the space between them. Choose plants that grow naturally in a geometric shape such as the conical dwarf spruce, or opt for shrubs such as yew or boxwood that can be pruned into spheres, cones, or any striking form you like.

Putting a path on the diagonal is another way to make a small space feel larger. In addition to being longer than a line that intersects the garden verti-

THE RUNNING-BOND PATTERN OF THIS BRICK PATH LEADS THE EYE TO THE FOCAL POINT AT THE END OF THE LONG VISTA. THE CIRCLE AT THE INTERSECTION OF THE TWO PATHS ADDS STABILITY TO THE DESIGN, WHILE THE PLANTS SPILLING ONTO THE BRICK SOFTEN THE FORMAL LINEARITY.

cally, a diagonal line is dynamic, contributing a sense of movement and excitement to the design. Place a bench, arbor, or ornament at the end of the path to provide a pleasing view or focal point. Alternatively, you can have perpendicular garden paths converge in the center, and put an ornament such as a sundial in the middle. In this case, the paths act as arrows pointing to the center and help draw attention away from the garden's boundaries.

Zigzagging and looping paths also make a garden appear larger, especially if the paths connect with one another so that they follow the longest possible distance between two points. Grow shrubs or dense plantings between nearby paths to disguise their proximity. A small suburban lot will feel quite large if you're able to take a long walk within its perimeters. Enhance the journey by adding visual treats such as a statue, birdbath, or special plant that visitors can discover just around the corner. Deep within the garden, widen the path to create a small, plant-enclosed patio. In addition to making a space seem larger, paths that curve out of sight, beckoning

THE HAZE OF BLUE CATMINT AND ALLIUM SCREEN THE FLAGSTONE PATH SO THAT IT DISAPPEARS FROM VIEW AS IT TURNS THE CORNER, CREATING A COMPELLING SENSE OF MYSTERY.

the stroller to follow, add the important element of mystery to a garden.

Paths can link two different garden rooms, or they can act as visual boundaries between spaces. If a path moves from one garden room to another, you might want to consider changing the paving material to signal the shift. For example, put a narrow steppingstone path down the side of your house that changes to a wider flagstone path as it runs across the back of your property. If your house has brick facing, you could begin with a brick path near the house to link the house and garden, and then change the paving to fieldstone set in quarry dust when the path enters a more informal space farther from the house. In some gardens, a crossroad in the path is signaled with a change of paving material at the intersection.

Paving the Path

How you pave your path will affect both its appearance and the nature of the journey. Brick, paving slabs, tiles, and flagstone all provide a smooth surface for walking. They are ideal for formal gardens and for primary paths, such as one leading from the street or driveway to your front door, where you need a safe, comfortable surface for walking. If you'll need to shovel snow off the walkway, make it

a smooth, solid surface so you won't have to worry about dislodging bits of path as you shovel.

For a more casual look, or in places where you want people to walk slowly so they will notice special plants or ornamental highlights, make the path

A RAISED WOODEN BOARDWALK MEANDERS THROUGH THIS BOG GARDEN, KEEPING FEET DRY AS IT LEADS VISITORS EVER DEEPER INTO THE FASCINATING WORLD OF PLANTS THAT THRIVE IN MARSHY CONDITIONS.

narrow and pave it with steppingstones or other materials that create an uneven surface. The random surface will force people to step carefully, allowing them more time to observe garden details. You can add to the viewer's enjoyment by having the path curve so the view around the corner is a surprise. Not only will the curve slow the walking pace, but the garden and all its wonders will gradually unfold as visitors stroll through.

Some of the most beautiful paths are made of a mixture of materials. For example, if you like the idea of a mosaic design of cobblestones but don't want to walk too much on the uneven, bumpy surface, you could make a cobblestone design at regular intervals in the center of a flagstone path, or line the edges with the cobbles. Set wood rounds into a woodchip path for an interesting blend of textures, or set bricks into a gravel path to create a pretty pattern and color combination.

Another method for adding interest to an informal path is to remove an occasional paver and plant low-growing perennials in the spaces. See Chapter 4, page 53, for a list of suitable plants to grow between pavers.

The style of your home should dictate your choice of paving material, especially for paths near the house. Choose materials that complement the structure, creating unity between the building—

See Chapter 4, page 53, for a list of suitable plants to grow between pavers.

YOU CAN ADD INTEREST TO YOUR GARDEN BY USING DIFFERENT PAVING MATERIALS. HERE A STONE SLAB PATH INTERSECTS A CRUSHED STONE OR GRAVEL WALKWAY.

Options for Paving Materials

Aggregate stone—concrete path with binding stone exposed

Brick—expensive, but looks good in almost any garden

Ceramic tile—an excellent way to merge indoor and outdoor paving

Cobblestones—charming, but uncomfortable for walking

Concrete paving blocks—some are colored and shaped to resemble bricks

Fieldstone—informal way to link garden to surrounding land

Flagstone, slate, sandstone—colors vary depending on region where quarried

Granite blocks—great for Japanese-style gardens

Grass—requires a clean-cut edge to look tidy

Gravel—must be edged so it doesn't spread into garden beds

Interlocking pavers—available in a range of colors and interlocking patterns

Marble—elegant way to merge indoor and outdoor paving

Oyster and clam shells, crushed—traditional colonial paving material

Shredded bark or woodchips—attractive in woodland gardens, but must be replenished annually

Wood—raised boardwalks make wonderful paths through boggy areas

Wood rounds—a wooden variation on steppingstones

the most dominant feature in your garden—and the landscape. For example, if you live in a Spanish-style house, you might want to opt for terra-cotta tile to visually link the garden to your home. A clapboard farmhouse calls for more informal paving, while a traditional colonial home will probably look better with paths made of brick or another formal type of material. Your goal is to have your home and landscape work together as a harmonious whole.

Giving a Path Direction

When you are laying out paths, it helps to keep in mind a few guiding principles. First, you must choose where the paths will go. If you are starting from scratch, observe the normal traffic patterns on your property: These are the routes you probably want to pave.

Some paths will be major thoroughfares. Make them comfortably wide—at least 4 to 5 feet across—to allow two people to walk together side by side. Other paths are like maintenance roads; they are the routes you take from the garage or garden shed with the wheelbarrow. While you don't want to sacrifice design considerations, you want these paths to be as practical as possible. They should be wide enough to allow a garden cart or wheelbarrow to pass through, and should follow a route that makes sense when you're busy working. If these don't take you where you need to go, you'll be tempted to cut corners through a flower bed. Finally, you may want a narrow footpath, just wide enough for one person, to wander through a wild, untamed section of your garden.

In an informal setting, a gracefully curving path is a pretty sight. However, the curve needs to go around something. Otherwise, it looks out of place, and walking the extra distance is just an inconvenience. Loop a path around an existing tree, or plant a tree in the bend of the path to justify the curve. A flower bed is another great obstacle for paths to wind around. It provides a beautiful focal point and beckons visitors to walk around as much of the perimeter of the bed as the path will allow.

You may also want to consider running a secondary path, perhaps made of steppingstones, across a stretch of lawn where people need to walk. Everyone will appreciate having a solid surface to walk on, especially when the grass is wet. Apart

Keeping Weeds Out of Bark Paths

Use thick layers of newspaper as a barrier to keep weeds out of bark or gravel paths. Eventually the newspaper will break down, enriching the soil. In the meantime, weed growth underneath the barrier will be halted. Any weed seeds that do sprout in the decomposing bark will be shallow rooted and hence easy to pull. When you need to refurbish a worn bark path, put down another layer of newspaper before you spread the bark.

Gardeners are often warned that colored ink on newspapers is dangerous for the garden. Today, however, most printers use colored ink that is nontoxic. If you are concerned that the ink might be toxic, check with your local newspaper.

from being functional, the byway will add interest and a new focus to the garden.

Paths with an Edge

An edging not only gives a path a finished look but also adds structural soundness, especially if the path is made of a loose material, such as gravel, or is set in sand rather than concrete; paving without an edging of some sort has a tendency to shift sideways over time. When a path runs through a lawn or next to a planting bed, the edging also helps keep the grass and soil where they belong.

There is a wide range of edging materials available, including brick (laid horizontally, vertically, or set on end at an angle to produce a toothed effect), tile, wooden strips, concrete or reconstituted stone strips, heavy-duty metal strips, and landscape timbers. Use your imagination. A path in an informal seaside garden might look pretty with an edge of large seashells, while logs or the trunks of small fallen trees would make an attractive, natural-looking border for a woodland path. You might use stone unearthed from your garden to edge an informal walkway.

Don't forget that you can also edge a path with plants. For example, a mass planting of catmint, dianthus, a low-growing ornamental grass, or hosta creates a dramatic frame. Most flowering perennials will blossom once a year for just a few weeks. For flower color along the path for the entire growing season, opt for low-growing annuals that will bloom continuously until the first frost, such as wax begonias, sweet alyssum, impatiens, or portulaca. Allow the plants to spill onto the path to soften the hard edge.

SHREDDED BARK IS AN INEXPENSIVE, ATTRACTIVE OPTION FOR PAVING PATHS. HOWEVER, THE BARK NEEDS TO BE REPLENISHED ABOUT ONCE A YEAR BECAUSE IT GRADUALLY BREAKS DOWN INTO HUMUS.

Lay a Path on a Budget

The least expensive paving for a path is chipped wood delivered free of charge from tree-trimming. Although a woodchip path is attractive in woodland gardens, the wood eventually breaks down and must be replenished once a year. In addition, as the chips decompose, the soil beneath the path becomes extremely rich, making an ideal environment for unwanted weeds to sprout.

For a more permanent, low-budget path, consider paving with quarry dust. This is tiny rock chips and dust that are a by-product of the quarrying process. The color of the material depends on the stone quarried, but is usually a soft shade of gray. Depending on the length and width of the path, the project should only take a day or two to complete, and the cost will be a fraction of what you would pay for brick, flagstone, or most other paving materials.

SUPPLIES

NEWSPAPERS

QUARRY OR STONE DUST *(also known as quarry screenings)*

EDGING MATERIAL SUCH AS WOOD OR METAL *(optional)*

BRICKS, STEPPINGSTONES, OR FLAG-STONES *(optional)*

TOOLS

SHOVEL

WHEELBARROW

LEVEL

FLATHEAD STEEL RAKE

ORDERING YOUR QUARRY DUST

Quarry or stone dust is available from quarries. Look in the yellow pages under "Quarries" and call the various companies for bids. The price per ton may vary dramatically, so it pays to shop around. Generally the cost will be around $8.50 to $12.00 a ton, but delivery fees can add substantially to the final cost. Many quarries charge a nominal fee if you haul the quarry dust yourself; loaders on site will fill the truck for you.

To determine how much quarry dust you need for your path, first calculate the cubic yards of material you will need. To do that, measure the length and width of your path in feet and then multiply those two numbers together. Multiply that sum by .33 for the 4-inch depth specified in Step 1 of Building Your Path, opposite. The resulting number will be the cubic feet of your path. To translate that sum into cubic yards, multiply the cubic feet by .037. A cubic yard is approximately 1.7 tons of dust, so to determine the number of tons of dust you need, multiply the cubic yards by 1.7. For example, if your planned path is 40 feet long by 2 feet wide by 4 inches deep, multiply the first two numbers together to get 80, and then multiply 80 by .33

for the 4-inch depth. That sum is 26.4 cubic feet. Then multiply 26.4 by .037 to determine the cubic yards. The sum is .9768 or almost 1 cubic yard. You would need approximately 1.7 tons of material.

If you'd rather not fuss with the calculations, tell the quarry company the length, width, and depth of your path, and let them do the arithmetic for you.

BUILDING YOUR PATH

1 Mark lines on the ground indicating the boundaries of your path. Estimate the cubic footage of your path (the length times the width times .33 for the 4-inch depth), and then call a local quarry to order the appropriate amount of quarry dust. Then dig out the soil from the pathway to a depth of 4 inches. If the soil is good quality, move it to other parts of the garden. Dispose of undesirable soil either by tossing it in a remote part of your garden or by carting it away.

2 Line the sides and bottom of your path with thick layers of newspaper. The biodegradable barrier will be more effective against weeds if you use whole sections as a layer, not just one or two sheets. On a windy day, you can spray the newspaper with water to keep it from blowing away once it's laid. If you are going to install edging, put that in place next. A good, relatively inexpensive option is pressure-treated landscape timbers or boards. Other possibilities include metal strips, bricks, stones, concrete strips, or tiles. Wooden strips should be held in place with stakes.

3 Spread a 3-inch layer of quarry dust, using a flathead steel rake to level the surface. To avoid puddles, slope the path slightly so water will run off; use a level to get the angle right. At this point you can set in flagstones, bricks, or steppingstones to add interest to the path, if you like. (The depth of the first layer of quarry dust will depend on the thickness of the stones or bricks.) Arrange the bricks or stones on the quarry dust surface, wiggling them slightly to position them properly. When they are firmly in place, add more quarry dust between the spaces until it is level with the added bricks or stones.

4 Water the path to settle the material. Keep a reserve of quarry dust to fill in any spots that may settle over the next month or two.

PART TWO

Decorating GARDEN ROOMS

Garden accents, decorations, and even the plants you choose establish the style of your garden, often becoming hallmarks that set your garden apart from all others. While many decorative features serve as focal points or add structure and a sense of order to the design, all of them contribute to the garden's sense of time, place, and character.

A SPIRALING STONE WALL AND TERRACED FLOWER BEDS ENCIRCLE THIS LITTLE SUNKEN GARDEN WITH ITS CENTRAL LILY POND.

CHAPTER SEVEN

Furnishing a Garden Room

Furnishing your garden can be just as much fun as furnishing your home. In fact, many of the same principles of design and function apply. The chairs, tables, benches, and seats need to be in scale with their surroundings and to fit in well with other features. Comfort also needs to be considered. In a formal room, you may want elegant beauty at the expense of comfort, but in other spaces comfort may take precedence over all other considerations. For example, if you want to dine outside on warm summer evenings, choose chairs that are comfortable enough to sit in for several hours. You and your guests will treasure the time spent relaxing in the garden with a good meal and stimulating conversation.

Within a garden there are places where you may choose to have built-in seating. For example, you can incorporate benches into the sides of a deck or balcony or design a raised bed, pond, or low wall with a wide edge where people can sit. If you need a place to keep seat cushions or other outdoor equipment, consider making built-in seats that double as storage space: Attach a hinged lid to weathertight boxes built at a comfortable height for sitting.

Portable furniture also has a place in the garden. Keep some lightweight, inexpensive chairs on hand that you can move around easily and set up wherever the garden is looking its best at any given time. These chairs may not be great works of art, but you'll find them very useful.

Furnishing with a Sense of Time and Place

Fads and fashions come and go. Everything from clothes to garden styles has a particular look associated with certain eras. For example, an ornate cast-

A TABLE AND CHAIRS TRANSFORM THIS POOLSIDE PATIO INTO A DINING ROOM. SITUATED UNDER A TREE FOR FILTERED SHADE, IT IS AN APPEALING SPOT FOR DINING ALFRESCO, OR TO ENJOY A SNACK BY THE POOL.

iron table, bench, or chair (or a modern aluminum substitute) recalls the new metalwork technology that the Victorians used to such good effect in their garden furnishings. A classic stone bench takes the garden back further in time, while furnishings made of modern, high-tech materials establish a sense of both the present and the future.

Similarly, many regions of the country are known for distinct styles of garden furniture. The Adirondack chair—with its sloping back and wide armrests—is named for the mountains in northeastern New York State, and the Battery bench is indigenous to Charleston, South Carolina. Bentwood rockers are made by craftsmen dwelling in the Appalachian Mountains. Redwood furniture comes from the great forests of the West Coast, and furniture decorated with Spanish tiles evokes the Southwest or Florida.

Use your garden furniture to help set the time, place, and tone of your garden. The following are a few outstanding styles from the many types of garden furnishings that are available.

BENTWOOD FURNITURE ᳵ Although bentwood furniture is now made all over the country, it originated in rural parts of the South, Amish Pennsylvania, western New York, Ohio, and Indiana. Each region has its own distinct style, but the furnishings are all characterized by a pleasing combination of naturally formed and milled wood. Bentwood furniture is made by bending and nailing fresh, supple branches or suckers from trees around a preformed frame. The best wood for these charming, rustic creations comes from fast-growing trees such as willow, alder, and cottonwood. Craftsmen

generally use the wood that is locally available. In the South, for example, you'll find bent willow furniture, while Indiana and Ohio craftsmen usually make theirs of cottonwood or alder. Whatever the region or material, the best-made rockers are contoured to fit your body so you can sink into one with pleasure and sit comfortably for hours in happy contemplation of your garden.

BATTERY BENCHES ᳵ In the mid-1800s the J. F. Riley Iron Works in Charleston, South Carolina, began producing benches with wooden slats supported by cast-iron legs and arms. Although the benches are now produced by Geo. C. Birlant & Co., they are still cast from the original mold pattern. The ironwork is intricately decorated with fanciful designs representing South Carolina's indigenous flora and fauna, as well as an inverted parrot, fox, and hound. Named after the fortified waterfront in Charleston, the Battery bench lends a touch of southern grace and is especially at home in a traditional garden with brick walkways and formal features.

ADIRONDACK CHAIR ᳵ It is no accident that the Adirondack chair is so comfortable. In the early part of this century, its inventor, Thomas Lee, had his family test different combinations of angled backs and seats until he got it exactly right. Then he added the wide, flat arms to hold a cup or glass. He made the prototype for his family's home in Westport, New York, on the southwest shore of Lake Champlain. Local friends and neighbors asked for copies, and the design became known as the Westport chair. Lee gave one of his Westport chairs to

Harry Bunnell, a local carpenter, who added a foot rest and a storage compartment to the design. Bunnell filed for a patent in his own name and eventually sold hundreds of the chairs to fashionable camps and resorts in the Adirondack Mountains. As a result, the design became known as the Adirondack chair.

CHINESE CHIPPENDALE ❧ In the mid-1700s, when England was colonizing the Far East, public interest grew in anything Oriental. The well-known furniture craftsman Thomas Chippendale recognized the trend and created a line of Chinese-style furniture. The design, which featured chairs with a pleasing blend of fretwork backs and plain, straight legs, was an immediate hit, and the Chinese Chippendale style has become an enduring classic. Chippendale chairs and benches are historically suited to an 18th-century, colonial-style garden, but their clean lines make them attractive in almost any garden setting.

LUTYENS BENCH ❧ Sir Edwin Lutyens, the famous English Edwardian architect who designed the British embassy in Washington, D.C., also designed furniture. In the garden world, he is perhaps best known for a distinctive garden bench with scrolled arms and a sinuous back design that rises to a peaked curve in the center. Considered one of Lutyens' most elegant furniture creations, the original bench was created in 1902 for the garden of Little Thakeham in Sussex, England. Although the design is less than a century old, it is considered a classic and is used to make both expensive and budget-priced garden benches and chairs.

BENTWOOD FURNITURE

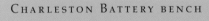

CHARLESTON BATTERY BENCH

ADIRONDACK CHAIR

GIVERNY BENCH ❧ Distinguished by an arching back and arms contoured to embrace the sitter, the Giverny bench offered in many garden catalogs is inspired by the benches that painter Claude Monet made for his famous garden in Giverny, France. Monet's benches, which were painted apple green to match the shutters of his house, were copies of ones he saw at the Hameau de la Reine, a garden created for Marie Antoinette on the grounds of the palace at Versailles.

CAST IRON AND ALUMINUM ❧ The industrial revolution opened up a new world of technology and building materials. To re-create the tone of a Victorian garden, choose ornate cast-stone or cast-iron furniture. If you cannot afford antiques, there are modern reproductions of Victorian garden furniture made of cast aluminum, which is lighter and more rust resistant than the iron.

Siting a Bench

Most gardens have room for more than one bench or seat. Even if you are too busy to actually sit in any of them, they add a touch of tranquillity and offer the opportunity for relaxation.

Put one bench at the end of a path to serve as a destination for strollers. Set a seat under a shady arbor or within an arch, and the spot will become a favorite retreat from the hot sun. Create a conversation circle in a courtyard to make a pleasant sitting room, or place one seat in a secluded, secret garden as a private spot to escape the demands of the outside world. For outdoor aromatherapy, find a place for a seat or bench in an herb garden or scented flower garden. Add a seat or bench to your front porch to create an inviting, welcoming scene. Finally, if you have a view, be sure to put a seat where you can sit and admire it.

In addition to functional considerations, think about psychological factors when you place a bench. Most people are uneasy if a seat is situated where they feel vulnerable. To create a sense of security, place garden seats in front of a wall or shrubbery.

You can visually anchor a bench to its setting if you give it a frame. Place potted plants on either side of the bench, set it within an alcove, or flank it with shrubs.

Your goal is to make the seat or bench an inviting, restful place where people will want to come for quiet contemplation or congenial conversation.

Issues of Color

Untreated wooden furniture that weathers to a soft gray or brown can be tasteful and blends beautifully with the garden environment. Sometimes, however, the furniture may be so well camouflaged that it disappears into the background, in which case it should be painted. Claude Monet painted his garden benches to match the green shutters on his house. By using color, he created a sense of unity between the house and garden, marrying the two in a happy, successful union.

PAINTED CINNABAR RED, THIS CHIPPENDALE-STYLE BENCH IS WELL SITED WITH A HEDGE AS A BACKDROP, POTTED TULIPS PLANTED ON EITHER SIDE, AND AN ATTRACTIVE VISTA IN FRONT.

Gardeners with a good sense of color can make a bench into a memorable, signature feature of their garden. With a good coat of paint, even inexpensive, mass-produced furniture can look special. Colors that look attractive on garden furniture include slate or Mediterranean blue, gray-green, black softened with a hint of green or blue, and Indian and Chinese reds. Choose a color for your furniture, and then use it as a theme throughout the garden on wooden planters, pots, or any other appropriate surface.

In addition to using the classic colors associated with garden furniture, many creative gardeners strike out in bold, new directions. For instance, you can create a special garden vignette by painting a seat to match or accent a nearby planting of flowers. Paint a chair a wine color to echo the blossoms of a honeysuckle vine, or choose an eye-popping royal purple to match a bold planting of annuals. If the color looks wrong, you can always repaint the seat.

White is a problematic color for garden benches. Some people feel that it is appropriate only in hot, sunny, seaside settings. However, there are many situations where white furnitue is lovely in the gar-

den. For example, a nicely styled white bench can be a delightful sight standing out against dark green foliage. And what could be more charming than a white seat under an arbor in a country garden surrounded by a white picket fence? Use caution, however: White can lighten a space, adding sparkle, but it can also dominate the scene and create a jarring effect.

Materials for Seats

The possibilities for garden seats are almost limitless. Carved-out logs, slabs of stone, and iron rods twisted to make a sculpture that doubles as a seat are

just some of the creative ways you can provide seating in your garden. Regardless of the design, however, most garden furniture is made of stone, iron, steel, aluminum, or wood.

Stone seats are beautiful but generally not very comfortable. Choose stone if you want to make a particular decorative statement, but don't put it in a spot where you'd like to spend a lot of time sitting.

Antique Victorian furniture is often made of iron or steel, which is heavy and prone to rust. The modern reproductions are usually made of aluminum, which can be shaped into the same intricate patterns as iron or steel but is more durable.

Wood is a versatile material for garden furniture and looks beautiful. Of the many kinds of wood, teak is among the most costly. However, garden furniture made of teak is a good investment because it is extremely resistant to mildew, wood-boring insects, and general weathering. In addition, it is a stable wood, so there is little or no warping or splitting. When left untreated, teak's orange color mellows to a beautiful silvery gray, which blends beautifully with any garden. Other durable woods for garden furniture include rot-resistant redwood, cypress, and red cedar. Pressure-treated lumber is not very attractive but is fine if you plan to paint the furniture.

SURROUNDED BY GOLDEN MARGUERITE DAISIES (*Anthemis tinctoria*), THIS CHAIR IS A WELCOME PLACE TO REST AFTER A SESSION OF DIGGING IN THE GARDEN. PUT CHAIRS AND BENCHES IN SPOTS WHERE YOU'LL ENJOY SITTING SO YOU'LL USE THEM MORE OFTEN.

CHAPTER EIGHT

A Room with Running Water

Water, an essential ingredient of life, makes a garden come alive. Whether it is a quiet reflecting pool or a gurgling fountain, a water feature draws people to its side. Somehow the presence of water in a garden touches us deeply. Still water is calming and peaceful; a gently flowing fountain soothes ruffled nerves and centers the soul; and the energetic splash of a large fountain or a waterfall is refreshing and dramatic.

Depending on the rate of flow and the terrain, water can ripple over pebbles, crash from a great height, or move slowly and quietly around obstacles. By directing the flow of water over and around various surfaces, you can also create different visual patterns. For example, if you spill the right volume of water over a smooth edge, you'll get an almost silent, sheer ribbon of water. Cut small, regular ridges into the edge, and the water will cascade in broken threads. A smooth, flat span of water gives the impression of space, stretching the horizon and acting as a mirror reflecting the surrounding environment.

Waterfalls and streams open up an exciting range of design possibilities. If you shoot water from a high spout so that the water lands on rocks below,

LEFT: BUILT INTO THE WALL, THIS GARDEN WATERFALL AND NARROW POOL TAKE UP VERY LITTLE SPACE. TOP: AN OLD MILLSTONE ADAPTS BEAUTIFULLY AS A GARDEN FOUNTAIN.

the droplets will splinter into a fine mist that refracts the sunlight, creating rainbows. Use a boulder to split a smooth-running stream into two smaller ribbons of flowing water, or dot a streambed with boulders, forcing the water to dance its way around each obstacle.

Ponds, pools, and other water features enchant. As Henry Mitchell, *Washington Post* garden columnist, wrote, "It's true that there are some gardens without fish pools, as there are some days without sunlight and some gardeners without the sense of sight or hearing. But let us pass over those tragedies and give the garden its potentially greatest jewel, ornamental water."

Designing A Water Garden

Once you've decided that you want to introduce a water feature into your garden, you need to have a clear idea of what you want to accomplish. For instance, you may want a naturalistic pond that blends seamlessly with an informal garden. If the pool will be close to the house or in an urban setting, consider a design that echoes an architectural feature or style, thus linking architecture with nature. You may want to evoke the style of a different culture, such as the narrow waterways typical of Moorish gardens or the distinctive Japanese lily ponds. In a small, narrow space you can create the illusion of spaciousness with a long, narrow stretch of water

TOP: A BORDER OF STONES HIDES THE EDGE OF THIS PRE-FORMED POND. TOP RIGHT: LONG AND NARROW, THIS SWIMMING POOL DOUBLES AS A BEAUTIFUL REFLECTING POND. RIGHT: AN OCTAGONAL POND MARKS THE INTERSECTION OF TWO GARDEN AXES.

that reflects surrounding trees and plants. Before you make a final decision on the design, look at photographs of water gardens of all shapes, sizes, and styles to gather ideas. Then adapt what you like best to complement your garden space.

You don't need to break through concrete or other hard paving to have a pond on your patio. Instead, consider installing a raised pond. In addition to bringing the fish and plant life closer to eye level, you can design the edge of the raised pond to provide additional seating.

Like any garden element, a water feature should be in proper proportion to the rest of the landscape. Don't make a pond too small: It will either disappear into its surroundings or look silly. Before you start to dig, mark the outline of the pond with a garden hose, then stand back and try to visualize how this new feature will look in relation to the rest of the space. At this early stage, if it looks too small or too large, you can easily make adjustments. In the case of a raised pond, stack empty boxes to approximate the proposed size and shape.

Placement is important when designing a pool or pond. You need to keep in mind design factors as well as the physical requirements of the plants and fish. Most water plants are sun lovers, requiring a minimum of 6 hours of sunlight per day. With some plants you can stretch the limits and give them

about 4 hours of direct sun, but you'll pay the price with fewer flowers. Choose a location for your pool or pond that gets full sun. Avoid nearby messy trees that will litter the water with their debris. The decomposing leaves of some trees, such as laurel, rhododendron, holly, laburnum, poplar, horse chestnut, and willow, produce salts and gases that are toxic to fish. Other trees to keep away from ponds include cherry and plum, which are hosts of the water lily aphid.

Creating a Water Garden of Your Own

"Water gardening is the easiest kind of gardening if you start out right," says Charles Thomas, founder of the International Water Lily Society and owner of Lilypons Water Gardens, a mail-order business based in Buckeystown, Maryland.

Indeed, compared to the "olden" days, durable pre-formed pools and high-tech plastic liners have made the job of installing a garden pool relatively easy. Customized pools and ponds designed by landscape architects are a different matter, of course, but the supplies available at home and garden centers make it possible for homeowners to install a basic water feature themselves if they wish.

Once the water garden is established, with the proper balance of plants and fish, maintenance is minimal. "You have no raking, no hoeing, and no weeding," says Thomas. Certainly a pond requires

less work than a perennial bed or a lawn. Once filled, it also uses less water than the same square footage devoted to flowers or grass.

Creating a Container Water Garden

Water has been a feature of grand gardens for centuries, but you don't need a sprawling estate and a king-size budget to have a water garden. In fact, the latest trend in water gardening is tub or container gardens, which are ideally suited for patios, decks, and small garden plots. All you need is a watertight container that holds at least 5 gallons and a spot that gets a minimum of 4 to 6 hours of sun per day.

The project is both easy and inexpensive, especially if you choose a reasonably priced container. Half-barrels or wine casks, which hold approximately 80 gallons of water, are superb for a large, rustic-looking water garden. Line the inside with plastic to prevent residue from the barrel's previous contents from contaminating the water. Some garden centers sell plastic liners designed to fit inside standard half-barrels, or you can staple durable plastic sheeting to the tub. Be sure the staples are above water level; otherwise, water may leak through the little staple holes.

Large terra-cotta garden pots make attractive water gardens, but they must be sealed because the unglazed clay is porous. Spray or paint the inside of the pot with at least two coats of urethane; allow the urethane to dry completely between coats. If you'd

A MOORISH STYLE POND WITH A MILLSTONE FOUNTAIN IS A BEAUTIFUL FEATURE TO DRESS UP A LARGE TILED PATIO. DROUGHT-TOLERANT LAVENDER AND STATICE IN POTS ADD GREENERY TO THE SCENE.

rather not fuss with waterproofing, choose fiberglass or plastic terra-cotta look-alikes. To plug the drainage holes, cover the outside of the hole with plumber's tape, then fill the hole from the inside with plumber's epoxy, which will form a firm, waterproof seal when it dries.

Other creative options for water garden containers include old, claw-foot bathtubs, galvanized horse troughs, metal tubs (line copper and zinc with plastic), and oversized antique kettles. Many water garden supply companies also provide containers for water gardens, including plastic half-barrels that look like the wooden originals.

You can devote your container water garden exclusively to plants, or include fish as well. If you opt for fish, select semitropical varieties such as gambuzi (mosquito fish), white clouds, swordtails, guppies, mollies, platys, killifish, and Chinese algae eaters. Compared to cold-water goldfish and koi, these fish are more tolerant of warm water temperatures that occur in containers kept outdoors in summer. If possible, position the container where it will get a few hours of relief from the hot afternoon sun. On a very hot day, add a few ice cubes to cool the water. The rule of thumb for the number of fish in a container is roughly 1 inch of fish length per gallon of water. You can push those limits if you install a small, submersible pump to circulate and aerate the water. At least one hour before you add the fish, treat the water with chloramine and ammonia remover (available from most pet

EVEN A TINY PATIO OR DECK HAS SPACE FOR A WATER FEATURE. WATERPROOF TUBS AS SMALL AS 5 GALLONS ARE ROOMY ENOUGH TO PLANT A CONTAINER WATER GARDENS.

shops or nurseries that stock water garden supplies).

With a submersible pump, or a pump discretely housed next to the container, you can decorate the garden with a small fountain. Fountain heads are available that create a wide array of effects. For example, there is a gusher that sends up a frothy, white column of aerated water. Depending on the horsepower of the pump, the column can be anywhere from 3 inches to a dramatic 24 inches tall. Other types of fountain heads include bubblers, tiered sprays, and a bell or "mushroom" jet that forms a smooth, clear dome of water. For your container garden, look for a small spouting ornament such as a frog, fish, or bird that you can perch on the rim of the tub, or choose a bubbler or small fountain head that rises out of the water.

Keep in mind that water lilies grow best in still water. However, if you have a large container, you could have a small spout of water flowing into the tub on one side and a water lily on the opposite side, as far away as possible from the moving water.

There is a wide selection of small water lilies and water plants that are ideal for container gardens. Choose a variety of plants; for example, one water lily, one Japanese arrowhead, one pennywort, and one bunch of *Sagittaria sinensis* would look attractive in a 100-gallon container. Use stacked bricks as plant stands inside the container so that each potted water plant is submerged at the appropriate level. To minimize the loss of water, opt for the large builder's bricks with holes.

Lilypons Water Gardens

Lilypons Water Gardens

WATER LILIES THAT STAY SMALL, SUCH AS *Nelumbo nucifera* 'CHARLES B. THOMAS', ABOVE LEFT, AND 'ALBERT GREENBERG', ABOVE RIGHT, ARE IDEAL FOR CONTAINER WATER GARDENS.

Add water to your container garden as necessary. If you don't have fish and the water level doesn't drop too low (that is, if you aren't adding more than 5 percent new water), you can use tap water without treating it.

In warm, generally frost-free climates, container water gardens don't require special maintenance over the winter. In the rest of the country, however, you'll need to plan for winter care. If your container is large enough, you can overwinter the hardy plants by floating a pond de-icer in the water and insulating the outsides of the tub with bales of straw or sheets of Styrofoam. Cut back any hardy water lilies. With care you can store tropical water lilies over the winter: Remove each plant from its pot and wash away the soil from the tuberous roots. Allow the tuber to air-dry at room temperature for about two days. Once it is dry, clean away any excess foliage and roots, then place the tuber in a jar of distilled water. Keep the jar in a

Plants for Container Water Gardens

WATER LILIES, HARDY

'Albatross', white

'Ellisiana', deep red

'Froebelii', red

'Gloriosa', red, takes semishade

'Gonnere', white, takes semishade

'Helvola', pale yellow

'Marliacea Carnea', shell pink, takes semishade

'Marliacea Chromatella', canary yellow, takes semishade

'Paul Hariot', scarlet, takes semishade

'Perry's Double White', white

WATER LILIES, TROPICAL

'Albert Greenberg', pink and golden yellow

'Colorata', pinkish blue

'Dauben', white with blue-tinged petals, takes semishade,

'Director Moore', purplish blue, takes semishade

'Leopardess', blue

'Mrs. Emily Hutchings', coral pink, takes semishade, night bloomer

'Mrs. John A. Wood', maroon, takes semishade, night bloomer

'Mrs. Martin E. Randig', deep blue

'Sir Galahad', white, night bloomer

'Tina Uber', amethyst

LOTUSES

Most lotuses are large, invasive plants. Here are a few dwarf varieties recommended for container gardens:

Nelumbo nucifera 'Charles B. Thomas', deep pink

N. nucifera dwarf Chinese varieties; pink, white, or red; grows 12"-24" high

N. nucifera 'Momo Botan', deep rose, leaves 12"-18" in diameter

N. nucifera 'Shirokunshi' (tulip lotus), pure white, grows 18" high

dark place where the temperature stays between 50° and 60° F. To get a head start on growth in spring, bring the tuber out of storage about two months before you expect warm summer weather to begin, and place it in water in a sunny window. Pot the tuber in soil when it sprouts, submerge the pot in 2 to 4 inches of water, and put it back in the sunny window. Bring the tropical water lily back outdoors when the water temperature of the container garden reaches 70° F.

The World of Water Lilies

Although water lilies look exotic, they are easy to grow. They also add immeasurably to the beauty of a pond. While a single blossom lasts only three to four days, water lilies will keep flowering from late spring through autumn (the hardy types will flower year round in frost-free climates), providing one of the longest seasons of bloom in the garden. The family of plants is divided into two categories: hardy lilies, which will

BOG PLANTS

Arrowhead *(Sagittaria latifolia)*, to 24" tall

Bog Lily *(Crinum americanum)*, to 24" tall

Horsetail *(Equisetum hyemale)*, to 18" tall

Iris 'Black Gamecock', blue-black flowers, to 18" tall

I. 'Clyde Redmond', deep blue flowers, to 24" tall

I. pseudacorus 'Flora Plena', double yellow flowers, 9" - 24" tall

I. versicolor, blue flowers, to 24" tall

Papyrus, miniature *(Cyperus isocladus)*, to 30" tall

Spider lily, variegated *(Hymenocallis caribaea variegata)*, to 24" tall

Spike rush *(Eleocharis montevidensis)*, to 12" tall

Square rush *(Eleocharis quadrangulata)*, to 24" tall

Umbrella palm, dwarf *(Cyperus alternifolius)* 'Gracilis', to 24" tall

SMALL, FLOWERING FLOATING AQUATICS

Floating heart *(Nymphoides peltata)*

Frogbit *(Limnobium stoloniferum)*

Passion plant *(Neptunia oleracea)*

Pennywort *(Hydrocotyle umbellata)*

Primrose creeper *(Ludwigia raepens)*

Snowflake, white *(Nymphoides cristata)*

Snowflake, yellow *(Nymphoides crenata)*

Water clover *(Marsilea quadrifolia)*

Water cress *(Rorippa nasturtium-aquaticum)*

Water hawthorn *(Aponogeton distachyus)*

Water hyacinth *(Eichhornia crassipes)*

Water poppy *(Hydrocleys nymphoides)*

OXYGENATING GRASSES

Ancharis

Cabomba

Myriophyllum

Sagittaria sinensis, miniature

Vallisneria

Make a Pot Fountain

Freestanding garden fountains are wonderful for cooling a formal patio or as a focal point along a garden path. When placed in a leafy glade or secret garden, a pot fountain adds motion and life to the secluded spot.

Setting up the pot and fountain is a quick, easy project. However, unless the fountain is right next to an electrical source, you'll need to run an electrical line from a ground-default outlet at the house to a junction box and outlet beside the fountain. You'll also need to bury insulated underground wiring at least 6 inches deep inside a plastic pipe. If you don't have experience with electrical wiring, you can save money on the electrician's fees by digging the trench from the house to the fountain yourself and buying all the required electrical supplies. If you do the wiring yourself, be aware of local county codes, and check with your utility company for the location of underground cables before you begin digging.

SUPPLIES NEEDED FOR FOUNTAIN

WATERPROOF POT—E.G., AN URN, A TALL STRAWBERRY POT, OR A LARGE AMPHORA *(seal with two coats of urethane if pot is made of porous material)*

SUBMERSIBLE PUMP

LENGTH OF TUBING *(long enough to reach from pump to water surface)*

FOUNTAIN HEAD *(optional)*

SILICONE SEALANT

ELECTRIC DRILL *(optional)*

ELECTRICAL SUPPLIES

INSULATED UNDERGROUND WIRE RATED FOR PUMP'S CURRENT REQUIREMENTS *(optional)*

³/₄" PVC PIPE *(optional)*

GROUND-DEFAULT OUTLET BOX

1 Before you begin, fill your chosen container with water (temporarily plug the drainage hole with tape, if necessary) and test the pump. You may need to experiment with the height of your water spout or fountain head and make adjustments accordingly. You don't want water to shoot up so high or a fountain to spray so wide that the water falls away from the container. As a rule, the mouth of the container should be at least twice as wide as the spray is tall. For a short, vertical jet of aerated water, set the spout just below the surface.

2 If your container doesn't have a hole in the bottom, drill one large enough to fit the pump's electrical cord. Run the cord through the hole, then seal it with silicone sealant (the container should be completely dry).

3 Place the submersible pump at the bottom of the container on a shallow base or stand (a brick platform works nicely). By raising the pump slightly, you minimize the likelihood that it will get clogged with debris that may collect on the bottom. Attach the spout to the pump's outlet pipe.

4 Fill the pot with water, turn on the pump, and enjoy.

5 Add water as needed to keep the container full, especially during hot weather or when rain is scarce.

grow in USDA zones 3 to 11, and tropical lilies, which are perennial in frost-free climates (zones 10 to 11) and can be overwintered in colder regions.

Hardy water lilies are daytime bloomers: On a sunny day the jewel-like flowers, which float on the water surface, open from midmorning and remain on display until late afternoon. They are often fragrant and range in color from white, pink, and red to yellow and orange. The flowers of some types change color as they mature. On the first day they open, for example, the flowers of 'Charlie's Choice' are a coppery orange; after that, they deepen to orange-red. 'Comanche' begins as a yellow flower with red flecks, then darkens to a golden orange on the second day; on the third day, it turns a deep orange-bronze-red. With just one plant, you can have three different flower colors all at the same time.

Tropical water lilies are all deliciously scented. The flowers stand well above the water surface, almost shouting, "Look at me!" There are both single and double forms in a wide range of colors, including pure blues and purples, pink, white, and yellow. Tropical lilies can be planted outdoors once the minimum water temperature reaches 70° F. In cold climates, they begin to bloom once they're exposed to 80°F for two to three weeks, and will continue flowering well into fall, usually about a month after their hardy cousins have shut down for the winter. There are two types of tropical water lilies: day bloomers, which open from about midmorning until late afternoon each day, and night bloomers, which

Make a Cobblestone Fountain

You can add an oasis to a drought-tolerant garden with a cobblestone fountain. This water feature is particularly effective at the mouth of a dry stone riverbed or as an accent in a gravel-covered area.

SUPPLIES

WATERPROOF TRASH BARREL

SUBMERSIBLE PUMP

LENGTH OF HOSE OR RIGID PIPE
(long enough to reach from bottom of trash barrel to a few inches above ground level)

METAL GRID OR STURDY WIRE MESH
(strong enough to bear weight; when cut into a circle, its diameter should equal that of the trash barrel plus, 2 to 3 feet)

PLASTIC SHEETING

SHOVEL

COBBLESTONES

WIRE CLIPPERS

1 Dig a hole deep and wide enough to bury the trash barrel so the rim is at ground level. Contour the ground immediately around the hole so there is a slight incline toward the hole.

open at dusk and flower through the night until late the next morning. Plant some of each for 24 hours of perfumed floral delight. (The blue and purple flowers are only available in day bloomers.)

All water lilies grow best in still water with their roots submerged 6 to 18 inches. Some varieties are large plants that spread 12 feet or more, while others remain compact, spreading as little as 1 foot. When you select plants consider their ultimate size at maturity.

2 Bury the trash barrel, then place a collar of plastic sheeting around the rim of the barrel. Use enough so that the plastic also covers the sloping ground out to about 1½ feet from the rim. This waterproof sheeting will catch any water that sprays away from the fountain and direct it back into the trash barrel reservoir.

3 Place the submersible pump at the bottom of the sunken barrel on a shallow base or stand such as a brick. By raising the pump slightly, you minimize the chance that it will get clogged with any debris that may collect on the bottom. Connect the hose or rigid pipe to the pump's outlet pipe. Run the electrical cord out of the top of the barrel to an outdoor electrical outlet. Hide the exposed length of cord under mulch or plant foliage.

4 With wire cutters, cut a small hole in the center of the metal grid large enough for the hose or pipe to fit through. Feed the hose or pipe through the hole as you place the grid over the buried container. When correctly positioned, the hose or pipe should rise above ground level out of the center of the barrel. Fill the sunken reservoir with water.

5 Cover the grid and any exposed plastic sheeting with the decorative cobblestones (try to hide the exposed pipe or hose without blocking the hole). Now give your new fountain a "test run." The water should bubble out of the pipe onto the cobble-stones in a small spurt and then flow back into the reservoir beneath.

6 Add water as needed to keep the reservoir full, especially during hot weather or when rain is scarce. Designed for underwater use, the submersible pump will be destroyed if it is allowed to run dry.

CHAPTER NINE

Garden Structures

Many people think of gazebos and other garden structures as frivolous or extravagant. In fact, well-designed gazebos, arbors, bridges, and other structures add immeasurably to the beauty of a garden. Many even become trademark features. For example, the bright orange, arching Japanese moon bridge at the Huntington Botanical Gardens in San Marino, California, is remembered by all who visit that garden, and the laburnum walk is an outstanding feature of Rosemary Verey's garden in Barnsley, England.

In addition, garden structures perform practical functions. Gazebos provide a sheltered place to sit, and pergolas link two garden rooms with a dramatic passageway. Bridges may span water or simply cross a dip in the landscape. Arbors offer welcome protection from the bright sun without blocking the light completely.

Arbors and Arches

The exact definition of an arbor has changed over the centuries. Originally an arbor was a living bower created by trees or shrubs planted close together and trained to arch over so they eventually form a leafy ceiling. Today the term covers any sitting area with a partially covered roof, as well as structures—also known as arches—used to frame a doorway. (To add to the confusion, an arch can be rectangular in shape.)

Arbors built over sitting areas not only provide some protection from the sun, they also create a sense of intimacy and turn an ordinary spot into something special. Ideally an arbor should be covered with climbing plants, but even one left bare has a stark beauty enhanced by the ever-changing patterns of sun and shade cast by the trellis or beams that form the ceiling.

Both arbors and arches are natural supports for

ROSEMARY VEREY'S FAMED LABURNUM WALK IS CREATED BY TRAINING THE YOUNG TREES OVER METAL ARCHES. YOU CAN TRAIN ANY TREE OR SHRUB TO BEND WHEN THE YOUNG WOOD IS SUPPLE AND SOFT.

climbing plants. Some of the most dramatic garden scenes are of blooming roses climbing up and over an arch, or of wisteria blossoms hanging down through the framework of an arbor. Take advantage of any upright feature in your garden to indulge in "vertical" gardening, training climbers and creepers up the structure.

What you choose to grow will depend, in part, on the structural integrity of the support. Some vines, such as wisteria, are very heavy and need a sturdy prop. Among the many climbing plants used to grace arbors or arches are clematis, climbing hydrangea *(Hydrangea petiolaris),* passionflower

THIS PLAIN ARBOR IS PAINTED TO MATCH EXACTLY THE RED FLOWERS OF THE HONEY-SUCKLE 'DROPMORE SCARLET' THAT IS SCRAMBLING UP ITS POSTS.

Build Your Own Four-Sided Arch

You could order an expensive, custom-made arch from a blacksmith. However, for a few hours of labor and a few dollars' worth of supplies, you can make your own arch using materials that are readily available at home and garden centers.

SUPPLIES

FOUR PIECES OF $^3/_8$-INCH (#3) STEEL REINFORCEMENT BARS, ALSO CALLED "REBAR".

FOUR 8-FOOT PIECES OF GALVANIZED STEEL PIPE $^1/_2$ TO 1 INCH IN DIAMETER

TWO 4-INCH GALVANIZED STEEL WASHERS

1 BOLT $^1/_2$ TO $^3/_8$ INCH X 1 TO $1^1/_2$ INCHES LONG

1 NUT $^1/_2$ TO $^3/_8$ INCH

1 WOODEN FINIAL TAPPED TO FIT BOLT

TOOLS

LADDER

SLEDGEHAMMER

HACKSAW

PLIERS

MEASURING TAPE

(Passiflora), roses (good climbers include *Rosa* 'American Pillar', climbing *Rosa* 'Cecile Brunner', *Rosa* 'Gloire de Dijon', *Rosa* 'Madame Alfred Carriere', climbing *Rosa* 'Sombreuil', and *Rosa* 'Zephirine Drouhin'), canary bird vine *(Tropaeolum peregrinum)*, trumpet flower *(Bignonia capreolata)*, and honeysuckle *(Lonicera)*.

Arbors and arches are hardworking garden features. They add height to a design—a valuable asset, particularly if the garden is predominantly hori-

1 Mark the positions for the four vertical pipes. Make sure they are aligned properly, since your eye will quickly detect imperfections that will bother you for years to come. Using a small sledgehammer, pound the four 8-foot-long pipes into the ground until 6 feet are remaining above ground. (You'll need to stand on a ladder to reach the top of the pipes.) As you pound them in, make sure they remain straight by asking someone to check with a level at various times.

2 To calculate the length of the rebars, you'll need to bend the rebar to form an even arc, then measure the distance between two opposite vertical pipes. The length of each "half arch" will be this diameter, multiplied by pi (3.14) and then divided by 4. Add an additional 6 to 12 inches to the length, and cut the rebar with a hacksaw. You'll need four pieces of equal length. Mark each piece of cut rebar at the point where you added the extra inches.

3 Insert one rebar into a pipe until the mark you made indicating the extra length is aligned with the top of the pipe. Carefully bend the rebar to form an even arc. (If you prefer, you can draw a circle on the ground the same circumference as your arc and use the curved line as a guide to bend the rebar.) Repeat with the other three, pointing each piece toward the center. Sandwich the ends of the rebar between the two steel washers and secure them together with the bolt and nut. A finial is a great decorative finishing touch if you can locate one with large enough threads to match the bolt.

4 Plant vines, such as wisteria, honeysuckle, clematis, or passionflower, at the base of each pole and train them to grow up and over the arch. Place a statue under the arch as shown in the photograph *(below)*, or hang a basket planted with cascading flowers from a hook attached to the central bolt. A vine-covered four-sided arch also makes a marvelous canopy over the intersection of two paths.

zontal. In addition, an arbor covering a patio or an arch placed at the beginning of a straight path acts like a picture window, framing the view and directing the eye; place something of interest, such as a sculpture, a fountain, or a remarkable tree or plant, at the point where the eye will come to rest. Finally, arbors and arches are focal points, adding interest to your garden.

Pergolas

A pergola is like an open tunnel or corridor. The side "walls" consist of parallel rows of columns supporting a "roof" that leaves lots of gaps open to the sky. Originally created to support climbing plants, a pergola also serves as a shady sitting area or as a dramatic passageway between two garden rooms.

Just because a garden is small doesn't necessarily mean there isn't room for a pergola. In many cases, it is simply a matter of choosing the right size for the space available. In a very large space, for example, you might want a pergola that's 8 feet tall and 15 feet wide. In a tiny garden, however, the structure could be much smaller. The minimum height should be about 7 feet 6 inches—tall enough for an adult to walk beneath it without feeling cramped. Make it at least 5 feet wide so that two people can walk through side by side. Whether a pergola is large or small, keep in mind that the columns and roof beams need to be in proportion to the overall size of the structure.

The supporting columns for pergolas can be made of any number of materials, including stone, concrete, brick, wood, iron, aluminum, or even tree trunks with bark left on. Depending on the material and how it is used, the pergola may be formal or informal, contemporary or traditional. Whatever the look, make sure the roof and columns are sturdy enough to support the weight of heavy vines; a pergola that isn't covered with climbing plants looks bare.

Use arbors and pergolas to frame an attractive distant view. Here the arbor points to the pretty gazebo, creating a connection between the two garden spaces.

A variation on the pergola is the arched walkway or tunnel. Painter Claude Monet's famous walkway in Giverny, France, is made of a series of metal arches painted green. He grew climbing roses up and across each arch to make a colorful floral avenue that runs from his front door to the far end of the garden. Some gardeners create the same effect for less money by making arches out of polyvinyl chloride (PVC) pipe. Although not a traditional material for garden construction, it does offer important advantages: It never needs painting, and it never rusts or rots. If you grow vigorous vines over the pipe, most people won't even notice it.

In addition to building a tunnel, you can grow one. Plant an avenue of trees, and while the branches are still young and supple, train them to grow in an arch over the center. You may need a metal frame in the beginning to tie the branches in the correct position, but eventually they will harden to the shape you want.

Whether you opt for a pergola or a tunnel, locate it where it makes practical—as well as design—sense

AN EIGHTEENTH CENTURY-STYLE "NECESSARY" MAKES AN ATTRACTIVE GARDEN SHED. THE SHED AND PERGOLA ARE BOTH PAINTED CINNABAR RED TO UNIFY THE DESIGN.

in the garden. It is disappointing to walk through a tunnel or down a covered pathway, only to have it lead nowhere. Pergolas and tunnels must have a beginning and an end and lead to somewhere special.

If you have a small garden, think about putting a pergola or tunnel along the edge of the property. In addition to defining the border and providing a pleasant, shady place to walk or sit, the structure will give you some privacy, especially if the neighboring house overlooks the garden.

Bridges

A well-positioned bridge makes a delightful addition to a garden. It is a picturesque focal point as well as a compelling destination. When it spans a pond or stream, it allows a fresh perspective from above, and it adds to the beautiful reflections on the water.

There are many different styles of garden bridges. Most distinctive are the high-arching "moon" bridges associated with Japanese gardens. Designed so the other half of the full moon is created by the bridge's reflection in the water, these bridges symbolize perfection. At the other extreme in Japanese gardens is the flat bridge, made from wood or huge slabs of granite or other stone. Depending on the width of these bridges, they may be a straight, unbroken span, or they may zigzag across in sections that have been spliced together. These zigzag bridges are often features of Zen gardens and are designed to foil evil spirits that want to cross the water. Western-style bridges tend to have a less extreme arc but are still eye-catching garden elements.

Whether Oriental or Occidental in style, bridges range from formal and elegant—for exam-

PEAR TREES ESPALIERED ON THIS METAL PERGOLA ADD VERTICAL INTEREST TO A VEGETABLE GARDEN, AS WELL AS PROVIDE FRUIT FOR THE HOUSEHOLD. NOTICE HOW THE ARCH IS ECHOED IN THE BRICK WALL.

ple, the gracefully arching creations with side railings decorated in the fretted Chippendale motif—to rustic and informal, such as those built from unmilled logs. In either case, the individuality of these bridges is often expressed in unusual designs for the side railings or banisters. When you are selecting designs for railings and finials, remember that the bridge should be in harmony with other features in your garden as well as the style of your house.

You can also add an individual touch to a bridge by painting it a distinctive color. As with garden benches, this is an opportunity to try out a color you might be uncomfortable using indoors. One option is to match the bridge to the color of the trim on your house, thus linking the two architectural features. Monet used this device in his garden in Giverny when he painted the bridge that spans his water lily pond green to match the shutters on his house. Another idea is to paint the bridge a color that picks up the color of nearby foliage—for example, the red of a Japanese red maple or the yellow of a shrub with golden foliage.

You don't need a pond or stream to justify having a bridge. If there is a low-lying drainage area in

THIS CHIPPENDALE STYLE BRIDGE MAKES A GRACEFUL CONNECTION BETWEEN THE TWO SHORES OF THE GARDEN STREAM AND STANDS OUT AS A BEAUTIFUL GARDEN FEATURE.

your garden, you can turn it into a special feature. Create a river of stones running the length of the dip, plant along the edges, then install a bridge over the dip. Depending on the other features in your garden, you may choose an arching bridge or a straight board or stone slab wide enough to walk across comfortably.

Whether crossing water or dry land, a bridge needs to be structurally sound, since people will inevitably want to walk on it. If the bridge spans wa-ter, be sure to add a support railing so that visitors can look down on the water and its reflections without worrying about falling in.

If you're handy with woodworking, a bridge can be a fun do-it-yourself project. Instead of going to all the trouble of bending wood into an arch, you can cut a 6-inch-deep arch out of a 12-inch-wide piece of wood. Calculate the desired curve of the arch and draw it onto the piece of wood starting at the bottom left edge of the wood for the low point of the arch. By

A STONE BRIDGE WITH AN EARTHEN SURFACE PLANTED WITH SHALLOW-ROOTED FLOWERS IS A BEAUTIFUL WAY TO SPAN AN INFORMAL STREAM.

the time the arch is at the center of the piece of wood, it should be at the top of the 12-inch width. Then it will slope back down to the bottom right edge.

Alternatively, many mail-order garden catalogs offer bridges delivered ready-made or in kits that are relatively easy to assemble.

Gazebos and Follies

The term gazebo was created by combining the words gaze and about. Indeed, gazebos are sheltered places where people can sit and gaze at the garden. For centuries, gardeners have wanted to do just that. Based on ancient paintings, it is believed that the first gazebos date back 5,000 years to the Egyptians, who built them in the royal gardens. These structures were placed at the intersection of waterways or under shady trees, and were valued as quiet, beautiful places for meditation.

In 15th-century England, when gardens were designed with intricate patterns created out of parterres, wealthy landowners built gazebos on top of walls. From this high vantage point, they could get a clear view of the ingeniously planted patterns. In the early 1700s, a few prosperous colonists in North America used gazebos as shelters from the hot summer sun. By the end of that century, gazebos were common features on American estates. Perhaps the best known of these is Thomas Jefferson's Monticello summerhouse, perched on the south-facing edge of his terraced vegetable garden. Just large enough for two chairs, the structure offers a commanding view of the 1,000-foot-long vegetable plot as well as a panoramic view of the tree-covered mountains around his property.

Once again gazebos are becoming popular in American gardens. They are available in a wide range of prices, styles, and sizes. Less-expensive models are offered in season at many discount warehouses; at

THOMAS JEFFERSON BUILT THIS PAVILION ON THE EDGE OF HIS TERRACED VEGETABLE GARDEN AT MONTICELLO SO HE COULD ENJOY THE PANORAMIC VIEW. HE CALLED THE MOUNTAINOUS VISTA HIS "SEA VIEW."

the other end of the spectrum are companies that specialize in finely crafted and even custom-designed structures.

Besides having potential value, gazebos make a beautiful focal point in a garden. For example, you can make a small garden feel larger by placing a small gazebo at the very end. The structure will attract the eye to the farthest boundary and serve as a destination, drawing people deeper into the garden.

Many gardeners install gazebos as pretty garden accents, but never actually sit in them. That's a shame, because gazebos are wonderful places for relaxing. Make yours comfortable so you'll want to spend time there. If mosquitos or other insects are a nuisance, consider installing screens to keep them out. Put comfortable chairs inside, and if there's room, add a table. At first, a gazebo may seem like an extravagance, but it could very well become your favorite place for drinks and meals alfresco.

When you add a gazebo to your garden, you are providing a new vantage point for viewing the scene. In most cases, the garden will look very different from this new angle. In a sense, you're giving yourself a second garden, so make it as pretty as you can. When you sit in the gazebo, study the garden and think about ways you can make the surrounding view even more attractive. Consider planting a vine with sweet-scented flowers, such as honeysuckle, near the gazebo to perfume the air. If you're likely to spend time there in the evening, plant night-blooming flowers or white

blossoms to enhance the nighttime display. You might even want to install a fountain nearby so you can enjoy the musical sound of falling water.

Temples, towers, and other structures that serve no practical purpose except as landmarks, distant focal points, or destinations for garden walks are known as follies. Created merely to delight the senses, these structures generally are located where they stand out in the landscape, such as at the top of a hill.

LEFT: THE SAD LOSS OF AN ANCIENT TULIP POPLAR TREE WAS AMELIORATED WHEN THE FAMILY BUILT A GAZEBO OVERLOOKING THE POND IN ITS PLACE. TOP RIGHT: A SCREENED GAZEBO IS IDEAL TO KEEP OUT INSECTS.

CHAPTER TEN

Lights in the Garden

Not so long ago, illuminating a garden for artistic effect was prohibitively expensive and complicated for the average home gardener. Wires for the traditional 110-voltage lights had to be carefully installed in waterproof conduits—a job that required the expertise of a professional electrician.

Today all that has changed. Low-voltage lighting systems, which operate on just 12 volts, are easy to install even for people who dread do-it-yourself projects. No special tools are required to set up the system, which usually takes less than an hour. It's not necessary to bury the wires (although you can), and the systems are designed so the layout can be easily modified if you change your mind or make alterations in your garden layout.

Low-voltage lighting has opened up a whole new world of decorative effects for the home gardener, and makes it possible to turn a pleasing daytime garden into a nocturnal place of enchantment.

Ornamental Lighting Effects

There are all sorts of beautiful effects you can create in your garden with artistic lighting. For example, you can use lights to showcase outstanding trees, shrubs, or ornaments, or to highlight special spots in the garden. The virtue of low-voltage lighting systems is that they are flexible and easy to move. You might want to focus on one plant in spring, when it is at the peak of beauty, and on another plant later in the year; it's not a big job to switch things around.

Here are a few ideas for transforming your garden into a beautiful nighttime scene:

IN BOTH SUMMER AND WINTER, OUTDOOR LIGHTING EXTENDS THE HOURS OF PLEASURE FROM YOUR GARDEN. DURING THE WARM MONTHS, A WELL-LIT GARDEN WILL LURE YOU OUTDOORS FOR LONG EVENINGS, WHILE IN WINTER YOU CAN ENJOY THE SCENE FROM INSIDE YOUR HOME.

MOONLIGHTING OR DOWNLIGHTING ☙
Floodlights pointing downward from high in the trees create the illusion of moonlight even on cloudy nights. Downlighting is particularly effective if the trees have a lacy canopy that casts an intriguing shadow on the ground. If placing lights in trees isn't convenient, put them high on a wall to illuminate objects from above.

UPLIGHTING ☙ Light pointing upward from the ground gives a new perspective on the world. Uplighting highlights bark and foliage and accentuates textures and forms. If you place the light right next to a wall and shine it directly upward, you'll get a grazing effect that picks out the surface texture and pattern of brick and mortar.

SILHOUETTING ☙ Shine a light from behind to make an interesting object stand out in silhouette. This lighting technique is particularly effective on a tree or shrub that has a simple, striking form with a well-defined outline. The plant will show up best if

SILHOUETTING

SHADOWING

MOONLIGHTING

UPLIGHTING

it is near a fence or wall, or in the open where there aren't other forms to distract from the silhouette.

Shadowing ‿ Double your viewing pleasure by shining a light in front of an object so that its shape is perfectly reproduced in a shadow on the wall or fence behind. Like silhouetting, this technique is most effective when used to highlight objects with a distinctive shape and outline.

Laying Out a Lighting Plan

To successfully highlight your garden at night with special lighting effects takes some thought and planning. Before you rush to the nearest home improvement center to purchase an all-purpose kit, take some time to think about what you want to achieve and which special features of your garden you would like to enhance.

Begin by assessing your garden during the day. Pick out one or two striking features such as a pretty pond setting, a dramatic specimen tree, or a statue, and then plan the lighting around them. Also, think about where you normally sit or relax outside. On warm summer evenings, you'll want to highlight a spot you can see from where you're sitting. For the winter months, choose a scene that looks pretty when viewed through a window from inside the house.

You probably don't want to light every tree and shrub in the garden. The positive, lit spots will be all the more special if they are seen in contrast to negative, dark areas. Also, don't throw too much light onto any one object or plant. Generally, subtle lighting is most effective. You want a natural look, such as moonlight filtering through the trees, rather than the brightly lit atmosphere of a parking lot. For variety, think about using different lighting techniques (see page 116) for different parts of the garden; if every single tree is given the same lighting treatment it will look very repetitive.

In most cases, lightscaping is most effective if you don't see the source of the light. If possible, conceal or camouflage the fixtures—for example, behind trees, bushes, or ornaments, or in flower beds. If you are putting lights up high, make sure they are angled so they don't shine unwanted or glaring light into your neighbors' windows or into the eyes of someone sitting or walking in your garden. Place ground-level lights where they won't get knocked down by the lawnmower or people walking by. Also, don't run wires where people could trip over them.

Low-voltage light bulbs that are on timers need to be replaced several times a year. That's not a big job if the fixtures are within easy reach. However, lights placed high in trees for the romantic moonlit effect are more work to maintain. When you settle on your design, be realistic about what you're willing to do to keep the system running.

If you are planning a combination of different light fixtures and effects, you may find it easier to visualize if you draw the scheme on graph paper. If you already have a site plan for your garden, use that. Otherwise, you can create a work sheet by drawing the outline of the house to scale and adding the other outdoor features. Don't forget to note the location of any outside, grounded electrical outlets.

Decide where you want to position each light,

and then work out the most logical and efficient layout for the cable wires. You'll need to consider the length and layout of each circuit, along with the total wattage of the lights, when choosing a cable and power transformer. Free do-it-yourself guidelines are available from outdoor lighting manufacturers to assist you in selecting the right equipment. Single box kits can be a less expensive alternative, but make sure they meet your lighting and layout needs before you purchase them.

Light Fixtures for Specific Effects

There is a wide range of low-voltage lighting fixtures, each designed to create a specific lighting effect. The list below will help you choose fixtures to create the effects you'd like to achieve in your nighttime garden.

WELL LIGHTS ✧ A well light is a spotlight housed in a weather-resistant tube. It is designed to be buried in the ground so the source of the light is hidden. Place well lights under trees and shrubs, to create uplit shadows and to highlight the undersides of leaves. They also work well along the foundation of a house, wall, or fence to accentuate textures and shapes.

FLOODLIGHTS ✧ Floodlights are wonderful for creating a multitude of garden lighting effects. They come mounted on a pivotal base so you can point the light exactly where you want it. Some are equipped with a focusing device that allows you to choose the width of the light beam, which ranges from a tight to a flood focus. In addition to providing added security, floodlights are great for artistic lighting. Use one to illuminate a fountain, sculpture,

or other special garden feature. Pointing downward from high up in trees, a floodlight looks like moonlight. For shadow lighting, put one in front of a plant growing against a wall or fence, and angle the light so the plant is illuminated and its shadow is cast on the backdrop. Position two or more floodlights near the ground, and angle their beams so they cross high above the subject. This technique sheds a pleasing, soft light on the objects, and adds depth and dimension to the scene.

TIER LIGHTS ✧ Mounted on a short post or stake, tier lamps are fitted with angled shades arranged in tiers. These shades direct the light downward so that pools of light illuminate the ground. Tier lights are ideal for lighting walkways and steps because the light is directed downward to provide safe footing without casting glare in anyone's eyes. These fixtures are also placed in a row along a terrace, like a necklace glowing in the night, or for highlighting flower beds and ground-cover plantings.

MUSHROOM LIGHTS ✧ Mushroom lights look like their namesake. A top cap conceals the light source and gives the fixture its mushroomlike appearance. As with tier lights, the lights point downward, making them useful for highlighting borders, walkways, and low-growing foliage.

BOLLARD LIGHTS ✧ Cylindrical in shape, bollard lights feature a faceted lens that diffuses light, making them useful for accenting walkways, flower beds, pool areas, and patios. Some come with a removable light shield, giving you a choice of full 360°

lighting or 180° in any direction. Bollard lights have a streamlined, contemporary look that is ideal for a modern-style home.

GLOBE LIGHTS ↬ Like lampposts, globe lights provide general, diffused lights. They are particularly effective when placed around swimming pools.

WELL LIGHT

FLOODLIGHT

SURFACE LIGHT

MUSHROOM LIGHT

BOLLARD LIGHT

GLOBE LIGHT

TIER LIGHT

Installing a Low-Voltage System

Once you've worked out your design, your hardest job is done. Putting the lights in is easy and takes only minutes. The only tools you need are a a screwdriver, measuring tape to measure the distance between lights, and a shovel if you plan to bury the cable.

1 Attach the low-voltage wires to the transformer box with the terminal screws and pressure plates provided. Make sure the wire insulation doesn't get in the way of the connection and that the terminals screws are tight. Plug the transformer into a nearby grounded outlet. You can leave the box loose or screw it to the wall with mounting screws. If the outlet is outside, the transformer box should be at least 1 foot above the ground with the cable terminals facing downward. Turn the transformer on.

2 Run the cable along the ground where you want to set your lights. If you need to tunnel under a paved path, attach a length of pipe to a hose with a pipe-to-hose coupling. Dig a hole on one side of the path deeper than the paving thickness. Then turn on the hose and use water pressure to create a tunnel under the path and out the other side. When the pipe protrudes from the opposite side of the path, attach the electric cable to the pipe and pull it back through. Then remove the pipe, leaving the cable in place.

3 Connect the lights to the electric cable following the manufacturer's instructions.

Most designs have an easy-lock system that snaps into place without any additional tools: Tiny teeth pierce the cable to make the connection. Since the wires are shockproof and the connecting holes are so small, you can move the connection and leave the old hole without creating a safety hazard or doing any harm to the system.

4 Place your light fixtures where you want them, measuring the distance between each if you want them evenly spaced. Well lights should be buried a few inches into the ground. If the light is mounted on a stake, simply push it into the ground by hand. Make any necessary adjustments, such as angling spotlights, so the light is cast exactly where you want it.

5 After you've attached all the lights to the cable and checked to be sure that the system is working, you can hide the electric cable under plants or mulch, or bury it. It's not necessary to dig a deep trench to bury the line; just make a cut in the soil or sod with the sharp edge of a shovel, pry up the soil a few inches, slip the cable inside, and press the soil back in place.

SURFACE LIGHTS ⁊ Surface lights have a compact, flat design so they can be mounted on the sides of decks and benches or along stair railings. They provide diffused light without glare and they lend a welcoming, festive feeling to a deck or stairway. You can also mount surface lights under eaves and along fences and walls.

Lighting for Security

In addition to being attractive, garden lights provide your home with added security. An intruder is going to be much less comfortable snooping around a well-lit property. Tier or mushroom lights illuminating the front walkway make the house more inviting to guests and less inviting to burglars. By the same token, a floodlight placed high above the garage door and activated by a motion detector is a useful feature for friends and family, but it makes unwelcome visitors wary.

Automatic timers that are set to turn on the outdoor lights in early evening and a few hours later give a lived-in look to the house if you are away. Another option is a photosensitive device that automatically turns on the lights when it gets dark and turns them off in the morning—an excellent choice if you want your house lit all night long.

IN ADDITION TO BEING DECORATIVE AND LIGHTING THE WAY INTO THE GARDEN AT NIGHT, A LAMP MOUNTED ABOVE A GARDEN GATE PROVIDES SECURITY.

CHAPTER ELEVEN

Ornaments to Embellish the Garden Room

Ornamental features in the garden perform several important design functions. With skill, you can focus a viewer's attention on an attractive sculpture, sundial, or birdbath, enhancing a pretty spot or perhaps even distracting from an unattractive corner you'd rather wasn't noticed.

Use ornaments to emphasize your garden room's strong features, as well as to expand or shrink the perceived size of the space. For example, if you place a small statue or urn on a pedestal at the end of a path, the path will seem longer than if you used a larger piece. A sundial or birdbath set in the middle of a small garden brings the focus to the center and minimizes the confining sense of nearby walls or fences.

Ornaments also lend a sense of time and place. Cast iron benches, urns, fountains, and sculptures hearken back to the Victorian age when breakthroughs in technology and manufacturing opened a new world of construction materials. Hand painted tile evokes the Mediterranean or Mexico, while a Japanese-style stone lantern transports the viewer to the Orient. Whether modern, classical, or Victorian, a large sculpture or urn helps create a sense of permanence and continuity in your garden room.

LEFT: PLACE A SUNDIAL AT THE END OF A PATH TO SERVE AS A CONCLUDING PUNCTUATION MARK. TOP: AN ANTIQUE WOODEN WHEELBARROW HAS A NEW LIFE AS A WHIMSICAL PLANTER.

There are people who have the gift of sifting through items in a junk shop to find the one perfect treasure. Part of their skill is realizing how something will look in a different context. In the right setting, well-positioned bric-a-brac can become charming. By the same token, even a valuable piece can look silly if it isn't well sited or doesn't fit into the overall garden scheme. All garden ornaments should be judged by their context and relation to the space around them.

Some people are so charmed with ornaments that they fill garden rooms with too many, making the space look cluttered. There are exceptions to every rule, but as a guide, try to have just one major ornament in view at any one time. Its singularity will enhance its importance and place in your garden.

Garden ornaments should introduce personality—your personality—into the garden. Don't be afraid to add a whimsical touch that tickles your funny bone or a keepsake that has meaning only to you and your family.

Sculpture

One of the nicest places to view statues is in the garden. Foliage acts as an effective backdrop to sculpture, and statues enhance the proposition that a garden is a special place—an Eden—set apart from the workaday world. As the renowned California landscape architect Thomas Church wrote, "After greenery, nothing, I believe, enhances a garden more than sculpture."

Whether the statue is a valuable antique, a modern, one-of-a kind work of art, or a mass-produced, inexpensive ornament, placement is key to its success. Ideally you should choose a spot in your gar-

PLACED IN THE NICHE OF A WALL, THIS SCULPTURE LENDS A SENSE OF ANTIQUITY TO THIS SIMPLE, CLASSIC GARDEN ROOM.

den that will show the piece off to good advantage as well as enhance the overall design.

Pale colored statues, such as those made of white marble or concrete, look lovely against a dark green background. Try placing one in front of a hedge of yew, boxwood, or holly at the end of a path—or prune a niche in the hedge to give it a custom-made frame. Less formal statues with simple lines and a minimum of adornment are attractive when surrounded with colorful perennials and annuals, or tucked into borders with a variety of foliage color and texture.

The eye is naturally drawn to interesting garden ornaments. You can use this to orchestrate how your garden is viewed. If you place a series of ornaments down a diagonal line in the garden, the eye will

Preventing Theft

Sadly, the theft of garden ornaments is on the rise. If you have any garden ornament you don't want to lose, protect it either by keeping it out of sight of the street, or by making sure it is securely fastened to something so it cannot be lifted and taken away. Thieves have even been known to cart away very heavy sculptures and garden furniture. Don't lull yourself into a false sense of security just because an item is heavy and awkward to carry.

SET ON EDGE, AN OLD MILLSTONE SERVES AS A MODERNISTIC SCULPTURE IN THIS FRONT GARDEN. BECAUSE THIS ORNAMENT IS VISIBLE FROM THE ROAD, IT SHOULD BE FASTENED DOWN TO PREVENT THEFT.

move along that line. In a small garden, place an interesting ornament at the end of a short path, and one's attention will be drawn to the garden ornament rather than the size of the garden. Tuck a small sculpture beneath arching foliage to create a whimsical vignette. Add a bit of intrigue to your garden by placing a statue at a bend in a path: The viewer will be drawn down the path to see what's around the corner.

Make sure your sculpture is in scale with its setting. To add visual importance to a small bust or statue, try placing it on a pedestal. A formal garden demands a traditional stone or molded concrete plinth; however, in an informal setting you could use a tree stump, stacked terra-cotta pots, or any other creative system you might devise to raise the level. Give a large sculpture a place of importance as the focal point at the end of a long avenue, pathway, or vista, or set it in the center of a pond.

Sundials

It is believed that the sundial was invented by the ancient Egyptians or Babylonians around 2,000 B.C. For centuries before the invention of clocks, the sun-

MOUNTED ON THE CAPITAL OF AN OLD CARVED COLUMN, THIS SUNDIAL IS SURROUNDED BY A LUSH PLANTING OF ROSEMARY, PURPLE BASIL, AND PURPLE SAGE.

dial was the primary way of measuring time. The mathematical knowledge for making sundials was passed to the Greeks during the heyday of their civilization, and from them to the Romans. It is from the Latin dies, or day, that we get our word "dial," since the sundial marks the twelve divisions of the day according to the sun's placement in the sky.

Sundials were traditionally placed on pedestals in the center of formal gardens: There they served as a central focal point and an attractive vertical element. They are equally at home in an informal, cottage style garden. Put one in the middle of a bed planted with low-growing flowers, or (if you like the idea of a pun) in the midst of a bed of thyme. Use one as a concluding punctuation mark at the end of a path, or highlight a flat expanse of lawn with a sundial. Inevitably visitors will be drawn to your sundial both to admire the design and to check on the time.

In addition to the horizontal sundials that sit directly on the ground or are elevated on pedestals, there are vertical sundials designed to hang on south-facing walls. If you have a bare expanse of wall that needs an ornament, consider gracing it with a sundial. Set off the ornament by growing a

Setting Accurate Sundial Time

A sundial displays solar, rather than clock time. In order to keep correct time, a horizontal sundial must be calibrated to your location. To do this, set the gnomon (the sundial arm that casts the shadow) so the upper angled edge (called the style) is equal to the latitude of your home. For example, San Diego, California is approximately 33 degrees north latitude. If you live in San Diego, use a protractor to determine the exact angle for 33 degrees, and then adjust the face of the dial until the style sits at that angle. If you don't know your latitude, find your town or city in an atlas or on a globe, and use the latitude lines to determine your latitude within one or two degrees.

If you live in the northern hemisphere, the gnomon, which is pointing to the number 12 on the face of the dial, must also face the north star, which is geographic or true north. (A compass points to magnetic north, which is slightly different.) To determine geographic north, first level the surface where you plan to set the dial. Then draw several concentric circles on the ground centered on the spot for the sundial. One circle will do, but if you make several,

you are not tied down to a specific time of day to take your measurements. Fix a dowel or stake into the ground at the exact center of the circles, making sure the stick is absolutely perpendicular to the ground. For a more accurate measurement, shave the upward end of the stake into a fine point.

In the morning, watch the shadow cast by the dowel, and mark the point where it touches one of the circles. Return in the afternoon and watch for the shadow to touch the same circle on the opposite side. If you make the first mark at 9 in the morning, (three hours before noon) you can expect the shadow to hit the circle on the opposite side at about 3 p.m. (three hours after noon). Mark the point where the shadow first touches the same circle on the opposite side. Draw a line between those two points, and then draw another line that bisects the first at right angles. Position the sundial so the gnomon points north along the second line.

Whether or not you choose to adjust your sundial for time-keeping in your latitude, acknowledge its original function and position it in a sunny spot.

BIRDHOUSE TUCKED IN TREE

CARVED STONE MORTAR FOR BIRDBATH

WHIMSICAL BIRD FEEDER

vine or espaliered shrub around the sundial, or flank it with a pair of trees or shrubs. With a little care, you can transform an unattractive wall from an eyesore to an asset.

Decorating for the Birds

It's especially wonderful when something that brings us pleasure also has a practical function. Attracting birds to your garden is beneficial both for insect control and the decorative interest of birds. Birds will flock to your garden if you provide for their three basic needs: food, shelter, and water. Fortunately, there are a host of ornamental garden accessories that will also meet the birds' needs.

BIRDHOUSES ✍ While many birds build their nests on tree branches, there are about fifty North American species that prefer to nest in a birdhouse. Each species has its own preferences for the size of its nursery, including the diameter and placement of the entrance hole and the floor space inside. For example, nuthatches, titmice, and downy woodpeckers prefer their houses with a 4-inch square floor and an 8- to 10-inch high ceiling. The entry hole needs to be 1 ¼-inch in diameter (except for nuthatches which need a 1 ⅜-inch opening). House wrens enjoy the same floor space as nuthatches, titmice, and downy woodpeckers, but seem to prefer less head room—a cozy 6- to 8-inch high ceiling. In either case, drill the entry hole 6 to 8 inches up from the bottom of the house, and position the birdhouse 5 to 15 feet from the ground.

If your birdhouse is honored with a bird, clean it out when the birds are finished nesting. Remove the nest and any collected debris, and then wash the inside of the house with disinfectant soap to kill any parasites that may be there. With luck, a new nesting pair will choose the house next year.

BIRDBATHS ❧ Water is essential for a bird's survival. Since they have no sweat glands, birds cool down by increasing evaporation in their lungs with rapid breathing. Because of this cooling technique, small birds are particularly susceptible to dehydration on hot days. They will fly for miles to find water, and are grateful for any source you can provide in the garden. In fact, a birdbath or garden pond will attract birds that otherwise might not visit.

From a functional standpoint, the ideal birdbath is no more than 3 inches deep with sloping sides, and has a rough or textured bottom so the birds won't slip. A light colored bottom will make it easier for the birds to tell that the water is shallow enough for drinking and bathing. If your birdbath is deeper than 3 inches, place decorative stones in the deepest part to make it shallower. The larger the basin, the more birds you'll attract. If there's enough space, several birds will bathe together, adding to the show. To be useful, a birdbath should be no less than 12 inches in diameter. One that's twice that size will attract more birds for a session of communal bathing.

When positioning your birdbath, choose an open spot in your garden, away from large shrubs and undergrowth that might harbor lurking cats.

BIRD FEEDERS ❧ Berry-bearing trees and shrubs in your garden will lure birds, as will a bird feeder stocked with seeds and nuts. Different birds prefer different foods. For example, sparrows enjoy grass seed, although occasionally they'll dine on

Multistory Birdhouses

Despite their charming appearance as garden accents, most birds will not nest in a multistory or "town house" style birdhouse. Territorial creatures, they prefer to keep significant space (an acre, if possible) between each nesting site. Purple Martins are the exception. These sociable birds, which are great to have around because they devour mosquitoes and other flying insects, prefer to nest in colonies of eight or more pairs in close quarters. High-fliers, they need apartment houses mounted 12 to 20 feet above the ground in an open lawn or meadow.

sunflower seeds. In contrast, the northern cardinal will spill seed out of a feeder in search of its favorite cuisine—unhulled sunflower seeds. If you have a particular local bird you'd like to lure to your garden, fill the feeder with its preferred diet.

Birds are messy eaters. Beneath your feeder you're likely to have uneaten grass seed sprouting, as well as a pile of cast-off hulls. Sunflower hulls, which are toxic to many plants, tend to make the ground barren where they fall . Keep these points in mind when you set up a feeder, and don't put one where you'll suffer more grief dealing with the side effects than the pleasure you'll experience watching the birds.

DESIGN CONSIDERATIONS ➳ Birdhouses, feeders, and baths not only attract birds, but are delightful additions to the garden. Place a garden accent for the birds where it will be an attractive focal point in your garden, such as at the end of a walkway. Put a birdbath or feeder on a pedestal in the middle of a flower bed, or use one as a vertical feature in a horizontal landscape. Tuck a birdhouse in a dark corner to lighten the area as well as to catch and amuse the eye.

Woven Magic

The traditional cone-shaped bee skeps made of twisted straw were once a practical garden feature designed to house honeybees. Their ornamental value was secondary to their purpose of keeping bees to pollinate the garden and orchards and to provide valuable honey and beeswax. Although charming as garden ornaments, bee skeps were an inefficient way to keep bees because beekeepers had to destroy the entire colony every time they harvested the honeycomb.

In 1851, a Philadelphia minister named Lorenzo Lorraine Langstroth invented the contemporary removable-frame beehive, and beekeeping was transformed. As a result, skeps are now used mainly as attractive focal points in the landscape, particularly when placed among aromatic herbs that attract nectar-seeking bees.

Plant supports woven from willow or reeds and shaped like teepees or pyramids are both useful and pretty. They add a helpful vertical element as well as an old-world, organic touch to a garden room. Use one to support vining annuals such as scarlet runner beans, sweet peas, moonflowers (*Ipomoea alba*), or morning glories (*I. imperialis*).

Putting the Accent on Sound

Wind chimes do double duty in the garden as ornaments and as a source of pleasing background sound. The pitch of the chimes depends on the length and diameter of each chime. You can choose chimes that tinkle like ice in a glass, enhancing the cooling effect of a breeze that sets the chimes in motion, or you can opt for chimes that produce a warm, rich cathedral sound. Some are a tuned collection of notes that produce harmonic chords used in different types of music—from Oriental, to Gregorian, Baroque, romantic, or popular. Try the power of musical chimes in the garden to transport you to another age or another part of the world.

Urns and Containers

Urns and containers are the workhorse ornaments in the garden. Use containers or urns in matched pairs to flank a path, doorway, or passage, or set a single urn at the end of a straight walkway to make a satisfying conclusion to the length of path. Although symmetrical pairing of objects is typically associated with formal gardens, this decorative motif works equally well in a casual or cottage-style garden. A pair of containers adds definition and extra allure to the prospect of the journey down the path.

Cluster containers in groups to make a more co-hesive and important statement than a single pot set down randomly here or there. This form of display is particularly effective if you're using inexpensive plastic planters. Clumped together, no one will notice or mind. It's also a winning technique to attractively fill in a blank space on a patio or deck.

Top: A traditional woven bee skep connects a modern herb garden to the past. Right: Willow or reed plant supports are a useful and attractive garden ornament.

Place containers in high spots, such as in baskets hung from tree limbs or house eaves, on wall brackets, or set on the top of piers that give structural stability to walls. Like layering plants in a shallow bed with tall specimens in back and shorter ones in front, this extra color adds immensely to a sense of rich planting and interest in a garden.

Choose your containers carefully to complement the style and sense of time and place in your garden. Large seashells make whimsical planters for shallow-rooted succulents in an informal garden, but may look out of place in a traditional or formal setting. Because they are made from a natural material, terra-cotta pots blend well in almost any garden. Stone, concrete, and cast-iron urns, whether antique or modern, recall the age of grand, formal gardens. Set them on pedestals to best show off their graceful, curving lines and patterns molded into the sides. Plastic containers shaped and colored to resemble clay or wooden counterparts are inexpen-

Above: Pots filled to overflowing with blooming flowers bring color and softness to paved areas. Right: Some pots, such as this tall amphora, have a sculptural beauty that shows off best when left empty.

sive and lightweight, but they lack the warmth of the natural materials they are imitating.

Natural Found Objects

Garden ornaments don't have to be man-made to be beautiful. Give your garden a sense of style with natural objects such as driftwood twisted and polished by the waves to resemble a modern sculpture, a local stone with a fascinating form, shells from the nearby seaside, or even old bones such as the animal

Planting Large Pots

Large pots make a strong visual impression in the garden, but they require an enormous amount of potting mix to fill, and then they are extremely heavy. Save money on soil and keep the pots lighter by filling the bottom with packing foam "peanuts" or any other lightweight, bulky material, and then top up with enough potting soil to give adequate space for the roots.

skulls that charmed the American painter Georgia O'Keefe. A well-placed natural object not only enhances the garden scene, but encourages viewers to appreciate the beauty in nature.

Using natural objects as ornament in the garden has a venerable history. The Chinese, who were among the earliest people in history to create gardens, graced their home landscapes with rocks that looked like animals. They named each natural stone "sculpture" after the creature it resembled such as "owl rock" or "dragon rock." These were given a place of honor in gardens that attempted to recreate the vastness of a wilderness landscape on an intimate scale.

Gazing Globes

Once popular in Victorian gardens, gazing globes reflect the surrounding plantings and sky in their shiny orbs. They look particularly effective standing on a pedestal (a birdbath plinth works admirably) in the middle of a cottage-style bed overflowing with blooming flowers. Children love to look into the sphere for an unexpected view of both flowers and sky.

Wall Plaques

Dress up an unsightly, bare wall with a frieze or wall plaque. These ornaments are particularly useful on north-facing walls that may be too shady and damp to successfully grow most plants. With increased demand for them, more and more specialty garden shops are stocking garden wall plaques. The very small plaques need to be hung on a small surface or surrounded by foliage. A good plant for growing on a wall is one of the many low-maintenance ivies that will tolerate both sun and shade.

A LARGE SHELL MAKES A BEAUTIFUL PLANTER FOR SHALLOW-ROOTED SUCCULENTS.

Weathervanes

Traditionally placed on the peak of the roof to predict the wind direction and assist in weather forecasting, weathervanes also make charming garden accents. Tuck one into a bed of flowers, or attach a small one as a finial on top of a lamppost.

Although they originated in Europe, it was in America that weathervanes reached their fullest development as works of art. With many of the early American settlers living a seafaring or agrarian life, they depended on knowing the direction of the wind, and the weather it would bring. At first the colonists imported weathervanes from Europe, but soon craftsmen began making their own designs, including Indians, horses and carriages, angels, ships, fish, birds, and any other motif that caught their fancy. Patriotic themes, such as the American eagle, became popular after the Revolutionary War. During the late 19th century, railroad, fire-fighting equipment, and other technological motifs reflected the national interest in industrial growth.

Choose a design that suggests something important to you or that communicates something special about your life. By placing a weathervane in your garden, you tap into a utilitarian craft that Americans have made all their own.

IN ADDITION TO BEING A COMPELLING FOCAL POINT, A GAZING GLOBE CREATES AN UNEXPECTED PERSPECTIVE ON THE GARDEN.

CHAPTER TWELVE

Plants As Ornaments

Some plants are useful as integral parts of the overall garden, providing a pleasing frame for other features. Other plants stand out as ornamental features on their own and can be used to create memorable effects in a garden room.

Think of plants not only as fillers, but also as potential ornaments in your garden. Some plants are remarkable in their own right; others can be trained to grow in fascinating forms that transform the mundane into something extraordinary. By incorporating specimen plants into your garden room and perhaps adding a specially trained espalier, topiary, or standard, you can create a decorated, landscaped space that is uniquely your own.

Outstanding Specimen Plants

Special features that distinguish specimen plants in the garden include a large size; an unusual or striking form; outstanding foliage color; and attractive bark, berries, and flowers.

Large Size

Sheer size can make a plant a sensational focal point. For example, an ancient copper beech tree with a

THE TALL, FEATHERY PLUMES OF PAMPAS GRASS (*Cortaderia selloana*), LEFT, ARE A DRAMATIC FOCAL POINT IN THIS FRONT GARDEN. MATURE SPECIMENS OF THE MORETON BAY FIG TREE (*Ficus macrophylla*), ABOVE, HAVE AN IMMENSE SPREAD WITH A MASSIVE BUTTRESSED TRUNK.

gray, wrinkled trunk that resembles an elephant's leg and wide-spreading branches graced with coppery red foliage is a stunning accent in the middle of a large lawn. Among the many other big trees that add a dramatic touch to a garden are cedar of Lebanon, deodar cedar, weeping willow, gingko, and red horse chestnut.

Old trees are a treasure. Apart from the character that age gives them, they add a sense of both permanence and a connection to the past. If you are fortunate enough to have an ancient tree in your garden, think about designing your landscape to make the tree an important feature or focal point.

Any plant that is large compared to most other members of its family is a candidate for a garden specimen. For example, ornamental grasses come in sizes ranging from the dwarf liriope, which makes an ideal edging plant, to the dramatic pampas grass (*Cortaderia selloana*), which grows up to 10 feet tall and produces soft plumes of feathery flowers that stand well above the fountainlike foliage. Although shorter, a large clump of *Miscanthus sinensis* is another good possibility for a specimen. In addition to the named varieties with solid green leaves, there are variegated ones such as *M.s.* 'Zebrinus', which has yellow or creamy white horizontal stripes, and others with longitudinal bands of pale cream or silver, including *M. s.* 'Variegatus' and *M. s.* 'Cabaret'.

Unusual or Striking Form

Many trees and shrubs have naturally contorted shapes that catch the eye. For example, many Japanese maples (*Acer palmatum*) offer delightfully twisted forms that contribute year-round interest in the garden. Their deeply lobed leaves are pretty in the summer and turn dramatic colors in autumn, and the bare branches make a fascinating silhouette in the winter landscape. Another plant appreciated for its unusual form is corkscrew hazel (*Corylus avellana* 'Contorta'). Also known as Harry Lauder's walking stick (for the bent, gnarled walking stick that was a trademark of the Scottish comedian Harry Lauder), the upright shrub produces long, drooping yellow catkins on the bare, twisted branches in early spring.

Many plants display a weeping or pendulous form that makes a dramatic statement in the landscape. In addition to the weeping forms of willow and cherry, consider some of the evergreen trees, such as Alaska cedar (*Chamaecyparis nootkatensis* 'Pendula'), Lawson's false cypress (*C. lawsoniana* 'Intertexta'), Brewer spruce (*Picea breweriana*), and the drooping variety of the blue Atlas cedar (*Cedrus atlantica* 'Glauca Pendula').

Some trees and shrubs have horizontal branches with spacing that creates a tierlike effect. One example is the pagoda dogwood (*Cornus alternifolia*), a deciduous small tree or large shrub that makes an attractive specimen plant in moist, partial shade. In spring the tiered branches are covered with small white flowers, which are followed by blue-black fruit. Another lovely shrub with tiered branching is the double-file viburnum (*Viburnum plicatum* var. *tomentosum*). Although it grows to only about 6 feet tall, it will spread as much as 10 feet, making a striking horizontal statement. Show off its unique features by giving it plenty of room to spread without being crowded by other plants.

Many conifers have striking growth patterns. For example, the Serbian spruce (*Picea omorika*) is a narrow, conical tree that resembles a church steeple when it reaches its mature height of 75 feet. The monkey-puzzle tree (*Araucaria araucana*) is a real conversation piece, with distinctly tiered branches and long, spiny needles.

Take advantage of plants with unusual or striking shapes by making them focal points and special decorative features in the garden.

Foliage Color

Golden yellow, silvery blue, and bright burgundy are just a few of the many foliage colors that occur naturally. Set against a background of green leaves, a plant with colored foliage will stand out as an ornamental feature. For red foliage, consider shrubs such as the red-leaf Japanese barberry (*Berberis thunbergii* 'Atropurpurea'), *Euonymus europaea* 'Atropurpureus', or *Weigela florida* 'Foliis Purpureis'.

Trees and shrubs with yellow or gold foliage include *Berberis thunbergii* 'Aurea', *Cornus alba* 'Spaethii' (variegated golden leaves), *Corylus avellana* 'Aurea', *Chamaecyparis lawsoniana* 'Lanei', *Cupressus macrocarpa* 'Goldcrest', *Cedrus deodara* 'Aurea', and *Taxus baccata* 'Aurea'. In regions that endure a lot of overcast days, golden foliage is a real asset because it adds a bright touch to the garden. In addition, the yellow color tends to come forward visually, serving as a beacon in gloomy weather.

Several conifers have striking foliage ranging from silvery blue to bright blue-gray, including *Picea glauca*, *Abies procera* 'Glauca', and *Cedrus atlantica f. glauca*. These plants, which often have a pleasing architectural form as well, show up beautifully against a dark background.

Japanese maple (*Acer palmatum*)

Golden thread false cypress (*Chamaecyparis pisifera* `Filifera Aurea')

Birch bark cherry (*Prunus serulla*)

Berries of heavenly bamboo
(*Nandina domestica*)

Pruned for an open form, this rhododendron makes a dramatic display.

Attractive Bark, Berries, and Flowers

A tree or shrub doesn't have to be a primary focal point 12 months of the year. For example, you might choose a plant because of its stunning bark that shows off to best advantage during the winter months, when the foliage is gone. In cold climates where gardens can look rather dull in winter, attractive or colorful bark is an important feature. For a change from standard brown bark, opt for red or yellow. As its common name suggests, the coral-bark maple (*Acer palmatum* 'Senkaki') has bright coral-colored bark that stands out in the winter landscape. Another maple, *A. pensylvanicum* 'Erythrocladum', has coral-red bark striped with silvery white. Tatarian dogwood (*Cornus alba*) is a small, multistemmed shrub with striking red twigs, while its cousin, the yellow-twig dogwood (*C.* 'Flaviramea'), has bright yellow winter shoots. In the birch family there is a wide range of bark colors, from the classic white to a brown, papery peeling bark that reveals pink and cream underneath. Some varieties of crape myrtle (*Lagerstroemia indica*) have beautiful bark streaked with green, gold, and pink, and the moosewood or striped maple (*Acer pensylvanicum*) sports green-and-white-striped bark.

Trees with peeling bark—regardless of the color—make lovely specimens. Look for the paperbark maple (*Acer griseum*), with orange-brown bark that peels off in thin flakes, or the Heritage river birch (*Betula nigra* 'Heritage'), which exfoliates at an early age and offers salmon-white and orange-brown bark. Both the buttonwood or eastern sycamore (*Platanus occidentalis*) and the London plane tree (*P.* x *hispanica*) are large trees with brown bark that peels off to reveal a trunk mottled in shades of brown, gray, and cream.

A holly tree or shrub covered with red berries is a glorious sight, and nandina brightens the winter landscape with its large clusters of berries that persist almost until spring. Pyracantha offers two seasons of dramatic display, with bountiful clusters of small, creamy white flowers in spring, followed by red berries that grace the plant into winter. Crab apples are lovely trees—ideal for small garden rooms— that bear a generous display of flowers in spring, followed by tiny, richly colored apples in autumn. Berry-producing plants make marvelous garden focal points in season.

Flowers make a cheerful addition to a garden room, and a tree or shrub that bursts into dramatic bloom is an especially welcome feature. A huge number of trees and shrubs flower in spring, offering a riot of color at that time of year. To extend floral interest in your garden, consider adding plants that bloom at other times of the year. Among the possibilities are hydrangeas (*Hy-*

drangea macrophylla, H. quercifolia, and *H. paniculata*), which have a long summer-blooming season, or the Rose-of-Sharon (*Hibiscus syriacus*), which bears trumpet-shaped flowers from late summer to mid-autumn. Cinquefoil (*Potentilla fruticosa*) also blooms throughout the summer. For blossoms very early in the season, try witch hazel (*Hamamelis x intermedia* and *H. mollis*), which flowers as early as January or February.

Annuals

Although frost tender, many annuals provide almost continuous bloom through the warm summer months. Delighted with this feature, the Victorians mass-planted the flowers to create colorful patterns and designs. Although still popular in theme parks and municipal plantings, the technique—called

A MASS PLANTING OF BEGONIAS MAKES AN EYE-CATCHING RIBBON OF COLOR ALONG THE EDGE OF THIS WATER LILY POND.

"bedding out" or "carpet bedding"—fell out of favor when Edwardian garden writers such as Gertrude Jekyll and William Robinson dismissed the designs as "ingenious monstrosities" and instead advocated more naturalistic plantings.

Nevertheless, if carefully planned, a massed planting of annuals makes a dramatic statement in a garden room. And because the plants die at the end of the season, you can try new plant and color combinations each year. For a little effort and only a few dollars, you can create entirely different looks in your garden with annuals—for example, a flashy blend of bold colors one season and a soft blend of pastels the next.

Well-Trained Plants

When trees and shrubs are young and their stems are still soft and supple, they can be trained to grow in a variety of shapes. Throughout the ages, gardeners have used this flexible quality to their advantage to create beautiful, and sometimes fanciful plant forms.

Unfortunately, many people today are either unaware of the possibilities for shaping plants or nervous about attempting such a project. In fact, training plants is not all that difficult. With a little effort and patience, you can experience the enormous satisfaction of creating works of art with plants.

Espalier

Espalier is the term for plants that are grown against a flat plane. The word comes from the Italian *spalla*, which means shoulder or support. An espaliered tree is ideal for a small garden because it takes up so little room. It is also a wonderful way to decorate an unsightly bare wall or fence. If you don't have a fence or wall, you can espalier a tree or shrub along

ESPALIERED TO RESEMBLE A CANDELABRA, THIS FRUIT TREE MAKES A DECORATIVE PATTERN AGAINST THE BARE BRICK WALL, AND IT TAKES UP VERY LITTLE ROOM IN THE GARDEN.

wires supported by posts. The trained plant will appear to be freestanding and become a living partition between garden rooms.

Almost any tree or shrub can be trained as an espalier, as long as you begin when the plant is young enough. Traditionally, fruit trees were espaliered along the walls of kitchen gardens. Gardeners discovered that the trees benefit from the extra warmth radiated from the walls. And by growing the plants vertically, owners can enjoy an extra harvest without taking up any significant planting space. As an extra bonus, espaliered fruit trees tend to bear 2 to 3 years sooner than trees planted in the open.

Other good candidates for espalier are forsythia and flowering quince (which lend themselves to informal, free-form training), southern magnolia (*Magnolia grandiflora*), cotoneaster, and pyracantha. In temperate climates, follow the lead of the Spaniards and grow oranges and other citrus fruits against walls.

You don't need a trellis to support an espalier, but it helps to have a system of wires laid out in the

Espalier Patterns

You can either train the plant into a formal design or grow a free-form espalier that is spread randomly on the wall and allowed to follow its own pattern. Choose a pattern that is well adapted to the natural growth habit of the plant you want to train. For example, magnolias, althaeas, forsythias, cherries, peaches, and plums grow in an upright form that suits a fan shape.

To train an espalier, begin with a young plant. If you can find an older plant that already has branches where you want them, that will save you time. Otherwise, purchase a year-old, unbranched tree, called a whip or maiden.

If you are beginning with a whip, prune off the end at the point where you want side branches to form. When the new shoots are long enough, choose two to train to the side and a third branch to train vertically as the central leader. (The exception is a Belgian fence, which requires just a pair of branches growing in a V-shape at a 45 degree angle.) Tie the side branches firmly, but loosely (you don't want to constrict the branches) at the angle you want them to grow. Since vertical growth is more vigorous than horizontal, branches that you want to train horizontally should be allowed to grow at a 45 degree angle their first summer. They'll grow faster, and they'll still be supple enough to bend into a horizontal position at the end of the growing season. Check the ties periodically to make sure they aren't too tight.

If you are training an espalier with multiple levels, allow the central leader to grow until it has reached the point where you want it to branch off again. Cut off the tip at a growth bud, and then repeat the training process for the new shoots that develop.

Once your espalier is established, trim back excess foliage along each branch so it looks neat and to keep the pattern clearly visible. To encourage abundant fruit or flowers, check the pruning recommendations for specific plants.

pattern you want to achieve. If you are training on a white wall, arrange the wires about a foot away to prevent any reflected heat from the wall from stimulating new growth too early in the spring. On dark walls that absorb heat, the wire supports can be as close as 4 to 6 inches. Do allow some space for air circulation, however.

Training an espalier will be a lot easier if you have a basic understanding of how pruning works. To put it simply, pruning is a way of communicating with the plant, telling it how you want it to grow.

Botanists have found that there is a concentration of a growth hormone in the tip of growing plants—a phenomenon called "apical dominance." When you cut a branch back to a bud, you redirect the growth hormone to the growing buds below the cut; every time you do this, the plant gets the message to send out shoots. The result is that every pruned branch will develop two or three new lateral branches that, in the case of espaliering, will be the next level in the pattern.

If you want to remove growth so it won't come

THE FAMOUS TOPIARY FOX HUNT SCENE AT LADEW TOPIARY GARDENS IN MONKTON, MARY-LAND, IS A WHIMSICAL MASTERPIECE. EACH YEW PLANT IS GROWING THROUGH A WIRE FRAME SHAPED TO THE ANIMAL'S FORM, MAKING ROUTINE PRUNING A MUCH EASIER JOB.

back, instead of cutting from the tip back to a growth bud, remove the branch at its growing source—either the tree trunk or the main branch. The message you deliver to the plant is clear: Don't send out extra shoots; there are enough here already.

The time of year you prune is important. If you want to increase the plant's vigor, prune in winter. If you hope to slow growth temporarily, cut back in summer. Exceptions to this rule are plants such as California natives that are dormant in summer and actively growing during the winter rainy season.

Topiary and Clipped Shrubs

Topiaries allow you to have a little fun and to introduce a whimsical touch to your garden. For example, you can prune a holly to resemble a large bowling pin, or shape a topiary into a fanciful bird. In the 1930s, Harvey Ladew created extensive gardens in Monkton, Maryland, featuring his now-famous whimsical topiaries, such as one of Winston Churchill's bowler hat and the "V for Victory" sign. The crowning glory is the topiary fox hunt complete with horse and rider jumping over a gate and following a pack of hounds in hot pursuit of a fox.

Geometrically trimmed shrubs are also considered topiary. Shape a pair of yew cones on either side of a gate into your garden to give a tailored look to

PINK STANDARD ROSES ECHO THE COLOR OF FRENCH IMPRESSIONIST ARTIST CLAUDE MONET'S HOUSE AND ADD HEIGHT AND RHYTHM TO THE NARROW FLOWER BED.

the entrance, or allow the end of a hedge to grow a little taller than the rest and then prune the extra foliage into a globe or pyramidal finial.

The traditional way to create a topiary is to trim a slow-growing shrub such as yew or boxwood into the desired shape. Some are created free-form, while more complicated shapes are grown in a wire frame used as a pruning guide. A newer approach to creating a topiary, which gets quicker results, is to grow a vine such as a small-leaved ivy or creeping fig (*Ficus pumila*) over a wire frame.

Standards

A standard is a plant that is trained to resemble a miniature tree. A dominant, upright stem is chosen

Create a Standard

You can train almost any plant with a woody stem into a standard. The list below includes just a few of the many plants that lend themselves to this treatment.

Begin with a young plant with a straight, central stem that has never been pinched. If there are multiple stems, prune away all but the central one you want to keep. The following instructions are for training a rosemary standard. The same principles apply for any plant, although shrubs such as lilacs or viburnums are trained on a larger scale.

Before you pinch the stem tip to create the bushy crown, consider the proportions you eventually want to have. The final height should be in balance with the size of the pot (if it is to be a potted standard) as well as the crown.

1 Insert an 8- to 10-inch-long stake next to the plant, either in the pot or in the ground. Remove side shoots along the plant's stem, but leave the primary leaves in place. Tie the stem to the stake at 1- to 1 ½-inch intervals, taking care not to damage the stem. As the plant grows, continue to tie the stem to the stake; when the plant outgrows the stake, replace it with a taller one. Also replace ties that have become tight as the stem grows.

2 When the plant approaches the desired height, pinch off the tip of the central stem. Allow the side branches near the top of the plant to continue growing; when they are about 4 inches long, pinch each of these just above a node to encourage vigorous, bushy growth. Continue pinching as needed to keep the head of the plant bushy and well branched.

3 Once the top growth has filled in, remove the primary leaves growing along the stem. Pinch or prune as needed to maintain the shape of the crown and to remove any unwanted sucker growth. As the plant matures, the woody stem will harden; when it is firm, you can remove the stake. Whether the standard is growing in a pot or in the ground, consider underplanting it with low-growing plants to carpet its "feet."

Plants Suitable to Train As Standards

Many of the plants listed below are not frost hardy. In cold climates, plan to bring frost-tender standards indoors during freezing periods; they'll make attractive houseplants. To help keep tender perennials healthy over winter, put them outside on days when the temperatures are above freezing. They'll appreciate the occasional exposure to fresh air and direct light. Just don't forget to bring them inside again if freezing weather is predicted.

Azalea (*Rhododendron*)

Burning bush (*Euonymus alata*)

Curry plant, dwarf (*Helichrysum italicum* spp. *siitalicum* 'Nana')

False heather (*Cuphea hyssopifolia*)

Fuchsia, upright varieties

Geranium (*Pelargonium*)

Lantana

Lavender cotton (*Santolina chamaecyparissus*)

Lavender, French (*Lavandula dentata*)

Lavender, Spanish (*L. stoechas*)

Lemon verbena (*Aloysia triphylla*)

Licorice plant (*Helichrysum petiolare*)

Lilac (*Syringa vulgaris*)
Mexican oregano (*Lippia graveolens*)
Myrtle, dwarf (*Myrtus communis* 'Microphylla')
New Zealand tea tree (*Leptospermum scoparium* 'Roseum')
Rose (grafted) (*Rosa*)
Rosemary (*Rosmarinus officinalis*)
Round-leaf mint bush (*Prostanthera rotundifolia*)
Sage (*Salvia officinalis, S. elegans*)
Sweet herb (*Lippia dulcis*)
Thyme (*Thymus vulgaris*)
Viburnum (*Viburnum opulus*)
Wisteria

as the leader. It is kept pruned so that the only foliage remaining is at the top of the plant, where it is allowed to grow like the crown of a tree. Normally the crown is allowed to grow free-form or is pruned into a sphere. For a more stylized effect, you can shape it to look like a mushroom, cone, or pyramid. Another variation is the "poodle," which features multiple balls or pompoms spaced along the stem at regular intervals.

The art of training standards dates back at least to the Middle Ages. Sixteenth-century Dutch gardeners used standards as vertical accents in their formal, very flat beds. Standards serve the same function in garden rooms today. Flank a doorway, bench, or path with a matched pair of standards, or set one in the center of a low garden to vary the height.

As the interest in this decorative form of plants grows, more and more nurseries are stocking plants trained as standards. However, it's not difficult to train your own, and you'll save on the premium price charged by a plantsman who has spent extra time and labor training the plant.

Knot Gardens

Knot gardens are made of different colored plants placed to create low-growing hedges that form a pattern of interlocking lines. It is believed that the original 16th-century knot gardens were inspired by the designs in Persian carpets.

An ivy geranium (*Pelargonium peltatum* 'Balcon Imperial') trained as a standard.

Today we often associate knot gardens with great estates, where there is plenty of space for a large garden room as well as a grounds staff to maintain it. While it is true that a knot garden requires precision to lay out, it doesn't have to take up a lot of garden space or be time-consuming to manage. For example, you could make a small, circular knot garden just 8 feet in diameter as a central feature in a formal garden room.

Traditionally knot gardens are created with shrubby herbs that can be pruned to maintain their shape, such as green and golden dwarf boxwood,

germander, lavender, lavender cotton, rosemary, and thyme. However, there is no rule that says you can't break away from that norm and use more unusual plants, such as sempervirens or other clump-forming succulents, low-growing annuals, or even leafy vegetables like spinach or lettuce.

Window Dressing

Windows are among the most neglected features in the garden. Indoors we pay lots of attention to dressing or draping them to soften their hard edges, and when necessary, to draw a veil of privacy.

Yet outdoors our windows are largely ignored;

Make a Small Circular Knot Garden

To be successful, a knot garden must be on level ground and laid out with mathematical precision. Use sand or lime to draw your pattern on the soil. To create the straight lines, stretch string between pegs; draw curved lines with a compass made by tying string to a peg.

Supplies

TAPE MEASURE

PEGS

STRING

LIME OR SAND

PLANTS

COLORED GRAVEL OR STONE

1 Find the center spot for your knot garden. Draw the outer circle to the desired diameter using a string tied to a peg as a compass. Then draw two lines perpendicular to each other through the center of the circle. To ensure that the second line is absolutely perpendicular to the first, make sure the length of segment "a" and segment "b" is the same as above.

2 Draw a square box inside the circle, with the corners of the box touching the outer edge of the circle. To be geometrically accurate, each side of the square should be equidistant.

3 Find the middle point of one side of the square, and use that point as the center for a circle the same diameter as the original circle.

4 Erase the lines of the circle outside the boundaries of the knot garden.

5 Draw three more arcs, using the central point on each side of the square as the center for the arc's radius. Plant along the marked lines, spacing the plants so they will touch and form an unbroken line when they reach maturity. You may choose to use three different types of plants: one for the square, one for the arcs, and one for the outer circle. Or you may want to keep it simple and use just one type of plant along all the lines. For added interest and to keep weeds at a minimum, fill in the blank spaces with colored gravel or stone.

the outside of our windows are sorely neglected, and we are missing out on a wealth of design opportunities as a result. For example, you can plant a clematis vine near a window and allow it to hang down on the panes to make a lacy screen. Add a whimsical "eyebrow" to a large window by training a climbing rose, wisteria, or honeysuckle up the side and across the top. Instead of wooden shutters, train ivy or a similar evergreen vining plant to grow around the window.

Raise color to a higher level and give yourself a floral view from both inside and out with window boxes packed full of flowers. Use a combination of upright and trailing plants, placing the cascading ones in front, where they can spill over the edge. (Provide excellent potting soil and keep the boxes well fertilized.)

You can add architectural importance to your windows by flanking them with tall, columnar shrubs, such as upright hollies. Keep the plants closely pruned to give the effect of pillars or miniature buttresses. For a more casual look, underplant the window with a colorful shrub, such as the red-leaf Japanese barberry (*Berberis thunbergii* 'Atropurpurea'). Allow a few branches to grow up past the window sill, providing a pretty view from the inside.

Extend your concept of outdoor window dressing to the garage door as well. Grow a vine across the top to enhance the blank expanse. Brighten the utilitarian spot with a pillar of geraniums, a flowering vine, or a pruned hedge flanking the door.

Whether you dress your windows to soften the lines, create a dramatic effect, add a whimsical touch, or provide color, your ultimate goal should be to make the outside just as compelling as the inside.

REFERENCES

Books

Beall, Christine. *Masonry*. Saddle River, New Jersey: Creative Homeowner Press, 1997.

Brenzel, Kathleen Norris, Editor. *Sunset Western Garden Book*. Menlo Park, California: Sunset Publishing Corporation, 1995.

Bricknell, Christopher and Zuk, Judith, D., Editors-in-Chief. *The American Horticultural Society A-Z Encyclopedia of Garden Plants*. New York: DK Publishing, Inc., 1997.

Brookes, John. *The Garden Book*. New York: Crown Publishers, Inc., 1984.

Eck, Joe. *Elements of Garden Design*. New York: Henry Holt and Company, 1995.

Erler, Catriona Tudor. *Trees & Shrubs* (Better Homes and Gardens Step-by-Step Successful Gardens series). Des Moines, Iowa: Meredith Books, 1995.

Erler, Catriona Tudor. *Herb Gardens* (Better Homes and Gardens Step-by-Step Successful Gardens series). Des Moines, Iowa: Meredith Books, 1995.

Felton, Elise. *Artistically Cultivated Herbs*. Santa Barbara, California: Woodbridge Press, 1992.

Gallup, Barbara and Reich, Deborah. *The Complete Book of Topiary*. New York: Workman Publishing Company, Inc., 1987.

Hayward, Gordon. *Garden Paths: A new way to solve practical problems in the garden* (Taylor's Weekend Gardening series). Boston: Houghton Mifflin Company, 1998.

Hessayon, Dr. D. G. *The Garden DIY Expert*. Waltham Cross, Hertfordshire, England: pbi Publications, 1992.

Hessayon, Dr. D. G. *The Rock & Water Garden Expert*. London: Transworld Publishers Ltd., 1996.

Hill, Lewis and Nancy. *Lawns, Grasses and Groundcovers* (Rodale's Successful Organic Gardening series). Emmaus, Pennsylvania: Rodale Press, 1995.

Hobhouse, Penelope. *Color in Your Garden*. London, England: Frances Lincoln Limited, 1985.

Jekyll, Gertrude. *Colour Schemes for the Flower Garden*. Woodbridge, Suffolk, England: Antique Collectors' Club Ltd. 1982.

Johnson, Hugh. *Principles of Gardening: The Practice of the Gardener's Art*. New York: Simon & Schuster, 1997.

Mack, David. *Making Rustic Furniture*. New York: Sterling Publishing Co., Inc., 1992.

McKinley, Michael. *How to Attract Birds*. San Francisco, California: Ortho Books, 1983.

Mulligan, William C. *The Lattice Gardener*. New York: Simon & Schuster Macmillan Company, 1995.

Nash, Helen and Speichert, C. Greg. *Water Gardening in Containers: Small Ponds Indoors & Out*. New York: Sterling Publishing Company, Inc., 1996.

Peterson, Roger Tory. *The Birds Around Us*. San Ramon, California: Ortho Books, 1986.

Robinson, Peter. *The Water Garden: A Practical Guide to Planning & Planting* (The Wayside Gardens Collection). New York: Sterling Publishing Company, Inc., 1997.

Seike, Kiyoshi; Kudo, Masanobu; and Engel, David H. *A Japanese Touch for Your Garden*. New York: Kodansha America, Inc., 1980.

Smith, Linda Joan. *Garden Ornament* (Smith & Hawken). New York: Workman Publishing, 1998.

Stevens, David. *The Outdoor Room.* London: Frances Lincoln Limited, 1994.

Strong, Roy. *The Garden Trellis.* New York: Simon & Schuster, 1991.

Thomas, Charles, B. *Water Gardens: How to Plan and Plant a Backyard Pond* (Taylor's Weekend Gardening Guides). New York: Houghton Mifflin Company, 1997.

Verey, Rosemary. *The Garden Gate.* New York: Simon & Schuster, 1991.

Verey, Rosemary. *The Scented Garden.* New York: Van Nostrand Reinhold Company, 1981.

Wagner, John D. *Building Adirondack Furniture.* Charlotte, Vermont: Williamson Publishing Company, 1995.

Zeman, Anne M. *Fifty Easy Old-Fashioned Roses, Climbers, and Vines.* New York: Henry Holt and Company, 1995.

Periodicals

Baldwin, Debra Lee. "Like Water for Landscape." *San Diego Union-Tribune,* September 18, 1994.

Brick Industry Association. "Technical Notes on Brick Construction 29A Revised." 11490 Commerce Park Drive, Reston, Virginia 22091-1525. www.brickinfo.com.

"Espaliers: Edible Landscaping in 'No' Space." *Gardens for All News,* November 1983.

Jellicoe, Geoffrey. "Voyage Round the Water Garden." *The London Times,* June 12, 1993.

Lilypons Water Gardens catalogue. 6800 Lilypons Road, P.O. Box 10, Buckeystown, Maryland 21717-0010. (800) 999-5459.

Martz, Wendelyn A. "Water in the Garden: Many Moods, Many Designs." *Citi: Charlotte's Magazine of Fine Living,* Summer 1995.

Mitchell, Henry. "Watery Rewards." *The Washington Post Magazine,* May 2, 1993.

Reznik, Michael L. "Light Up Your Life—The easy, do-it-yourself guide for designing, installing and maintaining low voltage outdoor lighting systems." Vanity Press, 7700 Winn Road, Spring Grove, Illinois 60081-9698, Revised, June 1992.

Scher, Valeria. "Pond in a Pot." *San Diego Union-Tribune,* July 13, 1997.

Smittle, Delilah. "Build Your Own Pool." *Garden Gate,* April 1996.

Stapleton, Constance. "Espaliers Add Life to Garden Walls." Washington Home supplement, *The Washington Post,* June 13, 1991.

Swezey, Lauren Bonar. "A Little Water Music." *Sunset,* June 1997.

The Southern Gardener. "Easy Fountain Makes a Splash." *Southern Living,* March 1995.

Thigpen, Charlie. "Flea Market Fountains." *Southern Living,* June 1998.

Van Ness Water Gardens. "Water Visions" catalogue. 2460 North Euclid Avenue, Upland, California 91784-1199. (909) 982-2425.

van Sweden, James. "Gardens That Go With the Flow." Washington Home supplement, *The Washington Post,* March 23, 1995.

INDEX

Dedication

To Nicholas and Ashton Erler with all my love. cte

Acknowledgments

I would like to give special thanks to my husband, Jim, for all his help and to Washington, D.C., landscape architect Robert Bell for being so generous with his time and knowledge about building brick walls. Thank you also to Betty Williams for her quick and helpful response to my request for information on their titmouse birdhouse, and to Charles Thomas of Lilypons Water Gardens for his beautiful photographs of water lilies. I would also like to thank Intermatic Incorporated (Malibu Lights) for letting me use their excellent photographs of gardens at night.

Picture Credits

All photographs by Catriona Tudor Erler and James Walsh Erler, except the following: page 119, photos by Intermatic Incorporated; page 95, photos by Charles Thomas, Lilypons Water Gardens.